SEX

"Middle-aged men simply know too much for young women—about sex, about themselves, and about the world ... I couldn't bring myself to explain again who Sandy Koufax was."

—Pete Hamill

LOOKS

"They used to shoot Shirley Temple through gauze. They ought to shoot me through linoleum."

—Tallulah Bankhead, at 54

AGE

"I refuse to admit that I'm more than 52 even if that does make my sons illegitimate."

—Lady Astor

MEMORY

"First you forget names, then you forget faces. Then you forget to zip your fly, then you forget to unzip your fly."

—Branch Rickey

TURNING 50

William K. Klingaman is a historian who was doing just fine until his ophthalmologist told him he needed trifocals. He can use his new glasses to look back upon his many achievements, including having written an acclaimed trilogy of histories of the twentieth century and the popular *Turning 40* (Plume). He lives in Columbia, Maryland.

William K. Klingaman

TURNING

Quotes, Lists, and Helpful Hints

A PLUME BOOK

PLUME
Published by the Penguin Group
Penguin Books USA Inc., 375 Hudson Street,
New York, New York 10014, U.S.A.
Penguin Books Ltd, 27 Wrights Lane,
London W8 5TZ, England
Penguin Books Australia Ltd, Ringwood,
Victoria, Australia
Penguin Books Canada Ltd, 10 Alcorn Avenue,
Toronto, Ontario, Canada M4V 3B2
Penguin Books (N.Z.) Ltd, 182–190 Wairau Road,
Auckland 10, New Zealand

Penguin Books Ltd, Registered Offices:
Harmondsworth, Middlesex, England

First published by Plume, an imprint of Dutton Signet,
a division of Penguin Books USA Inc.

First Printing, August, 1994
10 9 8 7 6 5 4 3 2 1

Ⓟ REGISTERED TRADEMARK—MARCA REGISTRADA

LIBRARY OF CONGRESS CATALOGING-IN-PUBLICATION DATA:
Turning 50 / [compiled by] William K. Klingaman.
    p. cm.
  "A Plume book."
  ISBN 0-452-27033-2
    1. Middle Age—Humor.   I. Klingaman, William K. II. Title
  Turning fifty.
  PN6321.M47T88   1994
  808.87'354—dc20   94–1992
                                                       CIP

Printed in the United States of America
Set in Palatino
Designed by Eve L. Kirch

CONTENTS

Looking Toward 50 — 1

The Wisdom of 50 — 5

Interview with Dr. Jan Sinnott — 31

Happy Birthday! (Parties and Presents) — 37

Movies for a 50th Birthday — 53

Interview with Tom Peters — 57

The 50s in Hollywood — 65

Life Begins at 50 (Perhaps) — 77

Famous After 50 — 85

Where Were They at 50? — 87

People Who, If You Are 50,
   You Have Already Lived Longer Than — 91

Love and Sex at 50 — 93

From the Sixties to the 50s — 105

Bob Dylan at 50 — 111

Your Body at 50 — 115

Interview with Ellen Goodman — 125

Athletes at 50 — 133

50 Facts — 141

"No man is ever old enough to know better."
—HOLBROOK JACKSON

"How old would you be if you didn't know how old you was?"
—SATCHEL PAIGE

LOOKING TOWARD 50

Turning 50 is not what it used to be. No one thinks of 50 as old anymore, and even if they did, one might expect that former heavyweight champion George Foreman—still fighting and chowing down cheeseburgers by the score as he closes in on the half-century mark—would pay them a visit and disabuse them of that notion. As the members of the baby-boom generation (present company included) approach 50, it will doubtless become fashionable, even trendy, to be 50. We can expect an even greater host of products and services geared to the over-50 market, accompanied by assurances that we are all still young enough to enjoy whatever it is we are being offered.

Certainly we have far more reason to celebrate our 50th birthdays than did our ancestors. For instance, a significant percentage of the residents of ancient Rome, two thousand years ago, never reached the age of 50 at all.

And for those who did, Cicero informs us that old age was thought to begin at 46.

Still, this was definitely an advance over the Middle Ages, when middle age was reckoned to begin somewhere around the twenty-first year. Peasants who made it all the way to 30 were considered lucky, wrinkled, and very old. In *The Inferno,* Dante declared 35 to be the prime of life; after that, it was all downhill to hell and gone. As late as the seventeenth century, the average lifespan in the reasonably civilized nation of France was still only between twenty and twenty-five years, and most adults died somewhere in their thirties.

Things had improved somewhat by the start of the twentieth century, when the average life expectancy for women in America was 51 years old—and only 48 years old for men—and the notion of turning 50 obviously carried far more drastic implications than it does now, when we can reasonably expect to live well into our seventies and probably beyond. In fact, recent research indicates that today's average 50-year-old American male can expect to live another twenty-nine or thirty years, while the average American female can expect another thirty-two years.

It is also true that advances in medical science, combined with the constant exhortations from physicians, advertisers, and the media to adopt a healthier lifestyle, have moved the physical frontier of aging back nearly a decade. Perhaps Gloria Steinem was correct when she claimed that "fifty is what forty used to be," although if that were true, then forty is what thirty used to be—or vice versa, I forget which—and those of you who are turning fifty should actually run out (after a brief warm-up, of course) and purchase a copy of my previous book, *Turning 40.*

In any case, my research for this book and its predecessor has taught me that most people seem to regard turning 50 as a considerably less traumatic experience than turning 40. I suspect the difference is far more psychological than physical, although Sigmund Freud probably would not agree. The eminent Dr. Freud was convinced that people over the age of 50 were entirely too old for psychotherapy. He claimed that their personalities were fixed by 50, and that their minds lacked the "elasticity" required to adjust and grow any more; besides, they had lived so many years and had developed so many neuroses, psychoses, and sexual frustrations that their therapy sessions would go on forever.

Rubbish, I reply. Most of the 50-year-olds I know are significantly better adjusted than they used to be. At 50, most of us seem to have accepted the fact that we are no longer exactly young. Breaking through the barrier of 40 disabused us of that notion. We know we have wrinkles, but we just can't see them. Instead, we can relax and enjoy the benefits of the midlife passage. Children are grown or nearly so. No one expects us to win Wimbledon, compete with college kids on a basketball court, or swim the English Channel. And besides, we are too smart and too secure to show off.

So don't worry about turning 50. Instead, consider adopting the philosophy of former baseball player Mickey Rivers, who was always a better sage than a center fielder. "Ain't no sense in worrying about things you got control over," Mickey liked to say, " 'cause if you got control over them, ain't no sense worrying. And there ain't no sense worrying about things you got no control over, 'cause if you got no control over them, ain't no sense worrying about them."

THE WISDOM OF

50

For the first time in American history, both the President and Vice President of the United States are under 50. This means that you will not find any quotes from either President Clinton or Vice President Gore in this section, or in any other chapter of this book. We are going to take a chance and assume that you will not miss them one little bit.

You will find herein an assortment of observations from the famous and nearly famous, from Aristotle and Plato to Groucho Marx and Casey Stengel. Some celebrities have handled turning 50 better than others, but among the wide range of philosophies I hope there is at least one that expresses your feelings on the subject. And if anyone wishes to send a copy of this book to either Clinton or Gore on their 50th birthdays, they will probably be in a position to use a laugh.

"Now that I think of it, I wish I had been a hell-raiser when I was thirty years old. I tried it when I was fifty but I always got sleepy."

—GROUCHO MARX

"Fifty is a nice number for the states in the Union or for a national speed limit, but it is not a number that I was prepared to have hung on me. Fifty is supposed to be my father's age."

—BILL COSBY

"At fifty everyone has the face he deserves."

—GEORGE ORWELL

"It was after fifty that I seemed to have crossed a frontier."

—SIMONE DE BEAUVOIR

"After fifty a man discovers he does not need more than one suit."

—CLIFTON FADIMAN

"The years between fifty and seventy are the hardest. You are always being asked to do things, and yet you are not decrepit enough to turn them down."

—T. S. ELIOT

"First you forget names, then you forget faces; then you forget to zip your fly, then you forget to unzip your fly."
—BRANCH RICKEY

"At fifty a man can be an ass without being an optimist but not an optimist without being an ass."
—MARK TWAIN

"Liebnitz never married; he had considered it at the age of fifty, but the person he had in mind asked for time to reflect. This gave Liebnitz time to reflect, too, and so he never married."
—BERNARD LE BOVIER

"Everyone has talent at twenty-five, but the difficulty is having it at fifty."
—EDGAR DEGAS

"Age shouldn't be newsworthy in itself; but it is one more boundary for women to break. Probably women have advanced at least a decade. Fifty is now what forty used to be."
—GLORIA STEINEM

"Once a man's fifty, he's entitled only to make large and serious mistakes."
—NORMAN MAILER

"The post office has a great charm at one period of our lives. When you have lived to my age, you begin to think letters are never worth going through the rain for."

—JANE AUSTEN

"Fifty knows that power does corrupt; that there are as many bad Republicans as bad Democrats . . . and that you should be aware of the charming, the articulate, the charismatic, because there are no heroes."

—ANN FERRIS

"So here are at least two good things that middle age gives you: the inestimable boon of freedom, and the precious gift of laughter. What makes youth unhappy is its desire to be like everybody else; what makes middle age tolerable is its reconciliation with oneself. But frankness well becomes the man who is no longer young. I would sooner be a fool of twenty-five than a philosopher of fifty."

—W. SOMERSET MAUGHAM

"Raunchiness is what I do best, I suppose, and I enjoy it, but I have limitations."

—TINA TURNER AT 52

"Working hard is a young thing, and nobody is young forever, but how old is fifty-five? Or for that matter, how young is twenty-five?"

—WILLIAM SAROYAN

"I am not advocating that you be fifty-one if you have a chance to be something else, but, unlike Gary Hart and Zsa Zsa Gabor, most of us cannot choose our age."

—RALPH SCHOENSTEIN

"When I was young, I was told: 'You'll see, when you're fifty.' I am fifty, and I haven't seen a thing."

—ERIK SATIE

"Looking forward from age fifty is no bowl of blueberries, but looking back, and distilling lessons from things, is difficult to do without sounding like Polonius when he was loading down Laertes with bromides."

—GEORGE WILL

"Every age has its springs which give it movement; but man is always the same. At ten years old he is led by sweetmeats; at twenty by a mistress; at thirty by pleasure; at forty by ambition; at fifty by avarice; after that what is left for him to run after but wisdom?"

—JEAN-JACQUES ROUSSEAU

"At fifty, you know that if everything did not turn out as you had planned, it is not the fault of your parents. There are market forces at work."

—KAREN DECROW

"The basic question in middle age might be this: How can I live the rest of my life with a modicum of grace?"

—PETE HAMILL

"He that is not handsome at twenty, nor strong at thirty, nor rich at forty, nor wise at fifty, will never be handsome, strong, rich, or wise."

—GEORGE HERBERT

"Anyone who is not yet a man at twenty, is not married at thirty, and not rich at forty, is a complete ass at fifty."

—SPANISH PROVERB

Optimists

"From fifty-one to fifty-three I have been happy, and would like to remind others that their turn can come too. It is the only message worth giving."

—E. M. FORSTER

"Anybody fifty years old can outsing himself when he was seventeen."

—WILLIAM "SMOKEY" ROBINSON

"I am maturing. That's better than aging. You enjoy different things."

—TED TURNER

"In middle age, you learn to forgive yourself.... The damage of the past is done; nothing can be done to avoid it or to repair it; I hope to cause no more, and I'm sometimes comforted by remembering that to many people I was also kind. For good or ill, I remain human. That is to say, imperfect."

—PETE HAMILL

"Other actors won't play a man of fifty, even though they are fifty. In Hollywood, they scratch out 'fifty' and say, 'He is thirty-five.' This having to be young forever ... that's America, Hollywood, eh? I find most people are more interesting when they've lived a bit more."

—SEAN CONNERY

"They were not really old—they were only 50."

—EUDORA WELTY

"It's very good to be twenty, thirty, or forty—each generation has its nice aspect when I look back. But you become yourself at fifty in a sense that you can do things in a more satisfying way."

—YOKO ONO

"I really believe life comes together around fifty."

—GAIL SHEEHY

"I am embracing my fifties. When I was in my thirties, I was told, 'When you get to be thirty-five, you'll get fat.'

Then, when I got closer to forty, 'You'll be a wreck at forty.' Well, I keep waiting for all these negative things to happen, and thus far they have not. . . . I don't want to go back to being thirty-five. I'm glad some of those struggles are behind me and the bonus days are coming."

—NANCY WILSON

"I rather like being fifty. For one thing I revel in the probability that I will not in the future make much more of a fool of myself than I already have."

—CLIFTON FADIMAN

"Today I have a greater appreciation for the good, soft, quiet moments, and I try to stretch them as much as I can. I can go for lunch, say, with my women friends, something I could never do ten years ago; I used to consider doing something just for pleasure a waste of time."

—BARBARA WALTERS AT 50

"You take all the experience and judgment of men over fifty out of the world and there wouldn't be enough left to run it."

—HENRY FORD

"My thirst for life is keener than ever, and I find the 'habit of living' even sweeter than before."

—GUSTAV MAHLER

"I can't say which, come eventide,
More tedious I find:
Competing with the juvenile stride.
Or meeting the juvenile mind.
So I think it rorty, yes, and nifty,
To be with people over fifty."

—OGDEN NASH

● ● ● ● ●

"Old people are more interesting than young. One of the particular points of interest is to observe how after fifty they revert to the habits, mannerisms and opinions of their parents, however wild they were in youth."

—EVELYN WAUGH

"I think middle age is the best time, if we can escape the fatty degeneration of the conscience which often sets in at about fifty."

—W. R. INGE

"Some of you have hidden your Bibles in your trunk, because your age is in your Bible. Your mother has written it in there. So you lock it in your trunk. Because you've been telling everybody you're thirty and you know you're fifty!"

—"LITTLE RICHARD" PENNIMAN

"The majority of men getting up there in age—though there are refreshing exceptions always—seem to feel that they are the answer to every maiden's prayers. This rather harmless form of insanity seems to hit them hardest in the fifties. Let a man meet a little heart-shaped face and immediately it must be his. He may not be so good at golf, but he is confident that he can make any girl in par."

—LETITIA PRESTON RANDALL

"At twenty, a man feels awfully aged and blasé; at thirty, almost senile, at forty, 'not so old,' and at fifty, positively skittish."

—HELEN ROWLAND

"You're aware of the rings in your tree."

—JACK NICHOLSON

"Either you die or you move along."

—MICK JAGGER

"A man past fifty should never write a novel."

—WILLIAM THACKERAY

"It is unthinkable for a Frenchman to arrive at middle age without having syphilis and the Cross of the Legion of Honor."

—ANDRÉ GIDE

"He that has seen both sides of fifty has lived to little purpose if he has not other views of the world than he had when he was much younger."

—WILLIAM COWPER

"If you're fifty years old, you've probably owned so many cars you can't even remember all of them in order."

—ANDY ROONEY

"A man who is over fifty, as am I, is sure that he has only about twenty minutes to live, and it is natural, I suppose, that he should feel disposed to put his affairs in order, such as they are, to harvest what fruit he has not already picked up and stored away against the winter, and to tie his love for the world into a convenient bundle, accessible to all."

—E. B. WHITE

"At fifty, I think I may be growing up at last. . . . I have learned a number of difficult lessons the hard way, because I guess I was always so sure that I had a better plan. It is time for some humility, and for the realization that after all this time I really know very little about anything."

—ALI MACGRAW

"I think about my career ten years from now. Suppose I couldn't dance as well? Suppose I couldn't give the performance I've always given? I've heard what people say about James Brown. 'Oh, he's gotten fat, he's not as good.'

They *forget* how great you were. I want to leave people with a memory of my best. And then go on to acting, where you can be fat and still good."

—TINA TURNER

"I wish they'd let me go out and make a regiment of men who are fifty or older. They'd be the best darned soldiers in the world."

—VICTOR MCLAGLEN, IN 1941

"For the man of fifty, it is always third and long yardage, with a nearsighted quarterback."

—BILL COSBY

"I'll say this about middle age: it is full of fantastic surprises. You find yourself saying, 'I'm fifty-one,' and thinking, *'What? I'm what?'* "

—ROY BLOUNT

"The real sadness of fifty is not that you change so much but that you change so little. . . . My only birthday resolution is to change some of my habits every year, even if only for the worse."

—MAX LERNER

"If you are ancient or forty-five or fifty and have acquired enough money to go to a ball game, you cannot drive a car on a highway, which is very hard to do after forty-five, to drive on any modern highway and if you are going to stay home you need radio and television to go along for receipts for the ball club."

—CASEY STENGEL

"A man shouldn't fool with booze until he's fifty; then he's a damn fool if he doesn't."

—WILLIAM FAULKNER

"One's fiftieth year is indeed an impressive milestone at which one may well pause to take an accounting."

—JANE ADDAMS

"At thirty, man suspects himself a fool;
Knows it at forty, and reforms his plan:
At fifty chides his infamous delay,
Pushes his prudent purpose to resolve;
In all the magnanimity of thought
Resolves, and re-resolves; then dies the same."

—EDWARD YOUNG

"I think every man should put down his recollections of this obscene world before he is fifty. Why wait, as usual, until you are a mere garbage can of disintegrating colloids, with teeth gone, thirst gone and memory gone?"

—H. L. MENCKEN

"The question ought not to be, 'How old are you?' but 'What have you done?' and 'What can you do?' "

— CHARLES KURALT

"Many people never climb above the plateau of forty to fifty. The signs that presage growth, so similar, it seems to me, to those in early adolescence: discontent, restlessness, doubt, despair, longing, are interpreted falsely as signs of decay."

—ANNE MORROW LINDBERGH

Reprinted with permission from Hallmark Cards, Inc.

"The beauty of growing older is that you don't have to throw yourself around anymore."

—CARMEN DE LAVALLADE

"I don't share the idea that turning fifty is 'no big deal.' It is a big deal; it is a half-century. Just surviving until age fifty is a big deal. You're two-thirds through what can be expected for a normal lifespan. . . .

   "To a great extent I'm mellower. I've learned how to take criticism much more in stride. I think I've gotten my priorities straight—being able to discipline a life separation between work and play."

—DIANNE FEINSTEIN

"But there is some comfort yet. Fifty and I are at an immense distance."

—CHARLOTTE LENNOX

"He could hardly be called old at the age of fifty-three."

—FYODOR DOSTOYEVSKY

"The really frightening thing about middle age is the knowledge that you'll grow out of it."

—DORIS DAY

"At fifty, you realize that the world will not hold still for you, that unthinkable passages take place. . . . And so, I no longer reread Shakespeare's sonnets because they talk too much about time and age and loss, thoughts I can do nicely without, especially between midnight and dawn."

—RALPH SCHOENSTEIN

"Grow up as soon as you can. It pays. The only time you really live fully is from thirty to sixty. . . . Only the middle-aged have all their five senses in keeping of their wits."

—WILLIAM HERVEY ALLEN

"The body is at its best between the ages of thirty and thirty-five; the mind at its best about the age of forty-nine."

—ARISTOTLE

"I don't suppose anyone will be much interested in what I have to say this time and it [*The Last Tycoon*] may be the last novel I'll ever write but it must be done now because, after fifty, one is different. One can't remember emotionally, I think, except about childhood, but I have a few more things left to say."

—F. SCOTT FITZGERALD

"It seems extremely odd to be fifty. Somehow, I did not expect it. The idea of being fifty years old was linked in my imagination with such implausible events as disappearing on the way to the grocery store—things that never happen to me. Fifty seemed to be some place at the end of the earth, like Ceylon."

—JANE O'REILLY

"I've come to the point where I tell myself, 'Give yourself a break. No one else will.' "

—PAUL MCCARTNEY

"I am just completing my forty-ninth year. You are just beginning yours. It is the grand climacteric which sets the course of the rest of one's life, I am told. It has been a year of lost friends for me. Not by death but wear and tear."

—EVELYN WAUGH

"Middle age is when you're faced with two temptations and you choose the one that will get you home by nine o'clock."

—RONALD REAGAN

"The process of maturing is an art to be learned, an effort to be sustained. By the age of fifty you have made yourself what you are, and if it is good, it is better than your youth."

—MARYA MANNES

"The man who views the world at fifty the same as he did at twenty has wasted thirty years of his life."

—MUHAMMAD ALI

"Now at last we can admit to ourselves that we will never read *Das Kapital* or reread *Moby Dick*. Never master karate, visit Tibet, write the great novel. Never win the Congressional Medal of Honor, sleep with Vanessa Redgrave, go back and sock our old schoolmaster or commanding officer. Never get to speak French like a native, even a native of Brooklyn."

—ALAN BRIEN

"I'm too damned old to bail out."

—Chuck Yeager

"I remember when my grandmother turned forty-seven—I wept. Now it's a whole new world for women."

—Carol Burnett

"It is in his fifty-to-seventy phase that a man pulls in his ears, lashes down his principles, and gets ready for dirty weather. . . . The middle-aged, except in rare cases, run to shelter; they insure their life, draft a will, accumulate mementos and occasional tables, and hope for security. And then comes old age, which repeats childhood—a time full of humors and sadness, but often full of courage and even prophecy."

—E. B. White

"The worst thing anyone has ever said about me is that I'm fifty. Which I am. Oh, that bitch. I was so hurt."

—Joan Rivers

"I love the idea of fifty, because the best is yet to come. I am going to live to be one-hundred, because I want to, and I am going to go on learning. . . . This has been the best year of my life."

—Shirley MacLaine

"A man may love a fading mistress, provided she fade before his eyes; he gets accustomed to it. But would he love this woman if he saw her for the first time at the age of, let us say, fifty?"

—D. W. GRIFFITH

"She was not old yet. She had just broken into her fifty-second year. Months and months of it were still untouched."

—VIRGINIA WOOLF

"I looked great when I was twenty but I can't look that way at fifty, and I refuse to fall into that trap."

—ELIZABETH TAYLOR

"You look around one day and the ballplayers are younger than you are. That's a big thing. The people in commercials are younger than you are. Even the yuppies are going to have to worry about that pretty soon. When they look at the soft-drink commercials, they don't see yuppies anymore. The doctors are younger than you; that comes as a shock. Clergymen are younger than you."

—AVERY CORMAN, author of the novel *Fifty*

Grouches

"I am aging fast, I am tired of life."
                                    —Pyotr Ilich Tchaikovsky

"I refuse to admit that I'm more than fifty-two even if that
does make my sons illegitimate."
                                    —Lady Astor

"I am there. Five-oh. In fact, I have been for many months,
and every day I expect to awake with a sense of adjust-
ment: 'Hey, fifty isn't so bad once you get used to it.'
Trouble is, I haven't. It's not that I am angry or melan-
choly. It's more an irritation. Sort of a chronic low-level vi-
rus. For those of you cruising quietly toward this
two-score-and-ten marker, be forewarned, as I was not,
that fifty is more than forty-nine plus one."
                                    —Tom Brokaw

"At fifty you begin to be tired of the world, and at sixty
the world is tired of you."
                                    —Count Oxenstierna

"After the age of fifty we begin to die little by little in the
deaths of others."
                                    —Julio Cortazar

"Forty and forty-five are bad enough; fifty is simply hell to face; fifteen minutes after that you are sixty; and then in ten minutes more you are eighty-five."

—Don Marquis

"The only good thing about it is you're not dead."

—Lillian Hellman

"All in all, I've got all the problems of a middle-aged woman, along with all the problems of a middle-aged man."

—Christine Jorgensen, following his/her sex-change operation

"Weinstein lay under the covers, staring at the ceiling in a depressed torpor. Outside, sheets of humid air rose from the pavement in stifling waves. The sound of traffic was deafening at this hour, and in addition to all this his bed was on fire. Look at me, he thought. Fifty years old. Half a century. Next year, I will be fifty-one. Then fifty-two. Using this same reasoning, he could figure out his age as much as five years in the future. So little time left, he thought, and so much to accomplish."

—Woody Allen

"Of course, at fifty I was old. . . . There were no gradations of old anymore: fifty was as bad as ninety. Youth and age had become spatial concepts with a Berlin Wall between them."

—Anthony Burgess

"I have nothing but the embittered sun;
Banished heroic mother moon and vanished.
And now that I have come to fifty years
I must endure the timid sun."
—WILLIAM BUTLER YEATS

"Everyone who's fifty swallows a little pride."
—JEANNIE SEELY

● ● ● ● ●

"I look pretty good. I work out every day. I go every now and then and have a little work done. I'm not going to say I don't. I'm fifty-seven years old and everybody knows it. I try and look my best because I'm all I've got and nobody's going to look after me. I don't have a sugar daddy or a husband. I gotta earn my own way."
—BLAZE STARR

"Happiness is *not* on my list of priorities. I just deal with day-to-day things. If I'm happy, I'm happy—and if I'm not, I don't know the difference."
—BOB DYLAN

"Age and color are things I don't think about. It can be a real obstacle to assume I can't have something because I'm a black woman. Or to tell myself I'm too old for this or that. I guess I've broken some rules. I don't put limits on my life."
—TINA TURNER AT 52

"It's odd how people of fifty remain exactly fifty. She [Violet Dickinson] hasn't changed a hair for twenty years, which must be the length of our friendship. We take things up precisely as we left them; a year's gap makes no difference; we have had our intimacy; something or other has fused; & never hardens again."

—VIRGINIA WOOLF

> *"They mistook the number*
> *27 is a number so is fifty*
> *Fifty is a number so is twenty-seven*
> *They mistook the number."*

—GERTRUDE STEIN

"My friend Olga said to me, 'I have always lived in the present and in eternity; I have never believed in the future. Being twenty or being fifty is really much the same thing."

—SIMONE DE BEAUVOIR

"I don't think getting older has anything to do with being less beautiful. When I'm fifty, I want to walk into a room and stop conversation."

—CHERYL TIEGS

"It is absurd to believe that a man can conclude a life of battles at the age of forty-nine. . . . Not only have I not finished my job, but I often feel that I have not even begun it."

—BENITO MUSSOLINI

"You all of a sudden realize that you are being ruled by people you went to high school with. You all of a sudden catch on that life is nothing *but* high school. . . . class officers, cheerleaders, and all."

—Kurt Vonnegut

"Ye shall hallow the fiftieth year, and proclaim liberty throughout all the land unto all the inhabitants thereof: it shall be a jubilee unto you."

—Leviticus 25:10

"The young talk about sex. The middle-aged talk about business. The old talk about their operations."

—Pablo Jury

"My job continues to be not to be afraid of making a fool of myself, even though I am not fifty-five full years of age."

—William Saroyan

"From forty until fifty a man is at heart either a stoic or a satyr."

—Arthur Wing Pinero

"If ye live enough befure thirty ye won't care to live at all afther fifty."

—Finley Peter Dunne

"This is the year I begin to talk to myself, having previously been too busy to make my acquaintance. It is, in Arnold Toynbee's phrase, a time of Withdrawal-and-Return. It is a watershed year."

—CLIFTON FADIMAN

"I do not know if the days are dwindling to a precious few for me or if I will make it to ninety-eight like my grandfather. Nevertheless, at fifty I am convinced that we must live as if we're immortal."

—BILL COSBY

INTERVIEW WITH
DR. JAN SINNOTT

Dr. Jan Sinnott, a psychologist who teaches at Towson State University in Maryland, is one of the nation's leading experts on middle age and the midlife crisis. In a recent interview, Dr. Sinnott discussed the concept of the dreaded midlife crisis and the frequent tendency of people in their forties and fifties to change direction, both personally and professionally.

Q: Everybody tends to associate the term "midlife crisis" with turning forty or turning fifty. Is there such a thing as a midlife crisis?

A: There *is* such a thing. About ten percent of individuals will experience a midlife crisis. Most likely, the crisis comes when you can no longer believe the rock-solid, concrete things that you thought you could believe. Socially, it happens when you're living in a way that worked twenty years ago, but doesn't work now.

So you can suddenly be confronted with a number of things that no longer work anymore, that are falling apart. And if those things all happen together, and the person hasn't been doing his or her homework all along, here comes an exam and you blow it.

But most people are able to resolve things as they go along, before they reach the crisis stage.

Q: So the steps leading up to a crisis are fairly common, but most people are able to adapt somehow?

A: Yes. You have a switch in the way you think about the world and time. You begin saying, "How much time have I got left?" And you've also accomplished some things. So you know what you're good at, and some things that you've failed at and probably will never succeed at. I probably won't be a better gymnast today than I ever was.

Q: And I'll never write the Great American Novel.

A: Actually, that might happen for some people, because that skill can improve. But you begin to see time in a different way, and you've made certain decisions that close off certain options. I'm up to four children now, so that's going to close off the option of my ever living free and alone.

Q: That's interesting. I had drifted away from teaching after I finished my graduate work in the late seventies, so I could concentrate on my writing. But last year I decided to go back into teaching, because I missed it. So you do make that shift.

A: Yes. Notice that at first it was a matter of mastering the concrete elements of your field—the writing and the thinking—and focusing on things you do alone. And now you're getting interested more in the reality of how it interacts with other people around you.

Q: That's right.

A: And you've already mastered that first part, so that's not as interesting or as much of a challenge as something you've never done. And now here's something fresh.

Q: Do you find that as people get into their fifties, they get better at working with other people?

A: Usually, yes. And part of what we ought to be teaching people is how to work cooperatively, in team efforts. The whole culture is getting there, you'll notice. We're leaving the cowboy mode.

Q: Do men and women handle this midlife passage differently?

A: The concrete aspects are still quite different for a lot of people, because we have different rules for men and women in our culture. But men and women overlap more in what they do about this than they are different.

Everybody's interested at bottom in how to use the time they have left. Everybody's interested in mastering something different. Everyone gets interested in the shared reality with other people. But men and women tend to bring out the side of themselves that they haven't brought out before.

Q: Do you think we make too much of milestones like turning fifty?

A: It's a gradual process in reality, but the human mind has to have these cutoff points. Fifty is a nice clear number to hang stuff on, and it's neat in the culture to say, "Now, behave like a fifty-year-old."

Q: Did you have any problems turning fifty? Did it bother you at all?

A: Not really. Turning thirty was a problem, but forty wasn't interesting at all, except that I happen to like decades. When I hit another decade, I typically sit down and say, "What was the neatest thing that happened in the last ten years, and where do you hope it's going to go in the next ten years?"

Fifty was interesting in that a lot of other people would bring it up. I happened to recall that other people always did "croning ceremonies," where you were honored for being the wise woman at age fifty.

Q: Croning ceremonies?

A: Yes, you became a crone, a wise woman. Or a witch, which is a wise old woman.

Q: I didn't know they had croning ceremonies.

A: Yes, you can do rituals, and it's a lot of fun. Fifty is the age of wisdom in female-dominated cultures. If you survived that long, you were officially old.

Q: Do you have any advice to give people who are about to turn fifty?

A: Have a good time. Life keeps opening up doors. The important thing is to be part of the story. Drop preconceptions, because as John Lennon said, "Life is what happens while you're making other plans." There's nothing about any of these decades that's preordained for any of us.

But if there's something that seems important, a path that's calling you at that time, and you haven't answered yet, why not now?

HAPPY BIRTHDAY!
(PARTIES AND PRESENTS)

"Join me as I celebrate (?) my fiftieth birthday
and try to wrest a few last wretched glimmers
of daylight from the encroaching flood tide of
decrepitude, senility and ... I forget what the
third one was."

—ARTHUR NAIMAN

Fiftieth birthday parties tend to have a different flavor
than those at 40. There is still some rueful laughter, but
there's less of an edge to it. It is a time to step back and
sort through the patterns of your life, to celebrate the
achievements of a half-century. (Fortunately, your faltering
memory has somehow mislaid most of the failures.) It is a
time to remain curious and open to new experiences.

Hold the bouquets of black roses and the foam-rubber
tombstones. Instead, consider giving your new quinqua-
genarian (boy, that word sure makes you seem old,
doesn't it?) a copy of Avery Corman's novel *Fifty*, about a
divorced sportswriter approaching his 50th birthday while
searching for love, wealth, and the meaning of life. Con-
spicuous consumers might prefer a volume called *Great*

Buys for People over Fifty, by discount maven Sue Goldstein. Hypochondriacs, on the other hand, could spend endless hours poring over *The Johns Hopkins Medical Handbook: The 100 Major Medical Disorders of People over the Age of 50.*

Restless spirits at 50 should consult *What Are You Doing with the Rest of Your Life?* by Paula Hardin. Those who are looking ahead to yet another half-century could use their own copy of George Burns's book of wisdom, *How to Live to Be One Hundred Or More.* And if you're feeling particularly frisky and want advice on how to get a date after 50, check out *The Late Show: A Semiwild but Practical Survival Plan for Women over 50,* by former *Cosmopolitan* editor Helen Gurley Brown. (Gentlemen, you need to take a look at this one, too, for your own protection. You'll see what I mean.)

The most depressing aspect of your 50th birthday is likely to be the arrival, entirely unbidden, of a packet from the friendly folks at the American Association for Retired People. Through its remorseless culling of names from credit card applications, magazine subscriptions, and motor vehicle administrations, the AARP manages to uncover the birthdate of the majority (about 75%, actually) of American citizens who are at or near the age of 50. Once it has identified its prospective victims—really, the idea of retirement at age 50 is rather silly, isn't it?—the organization sends out its standard packets and invites us all to join for a modest fee of $8.00.

Still, that is not quite as bad as the traditional Swedish ceremony for turning 50. In that bleak Scandinavian land, the entire town traditionally turns out to pat you on the back on your 50th birthday. At dawn, cannons fire a salute to the occasion, and brass bands play under your window at breakfast. This is not exactly what you need at this time of your life, and may help to explain why Sweden has long experienced one of the highest suicide rates of any country in the world.

But happy birthday, anyway.

● ● ● ● ●

"Now he fits in with my antiques."
                    —JACQUELINE JACKSON, on her husband
                    Jesse Jackson's 50th birthday

"On my fiftieth birthday, two nice things happened: I didn't think once about Brooke Shields and I wasn't taken directly to intensive care."
                                        —RALPH SCHOENSTEIN

"I did not take my fiftieth birthday with nearly the tragic upset with which I had greeted my fortieth, ten years before. In fact, I was in a rather good humor that day."
                                        —ISAAC ASIMOV

"I am surprised to feel so elated. After all, when I was a girl any woman eccentric enough to actually announce, much less celebrate, her fiftieth birthday might as well have printed 'new hope for hags' on the invitations."
                                        —JANE O'REILLY

"In the Middle Ages, a particular pope was so deeply revered that once a year he paraded through Rome's streets

wearing a ridiculous hat to discourage excessive venera-
tion. In our children's eyes, we are always wearing such
hats, but especially on our fiftieth birthdays, when we
have long ceased to be young and are a long way from being venerable."

—GEORGE WILL

• • • • •

When Indiana University basketball coach Bobby
Knight turned 50 on October 25, 1990, nearly three thousand people attended a party in Knight's honor. Vice President Dan Quayle sent his greetings by video. "I'm only
sorry I couldn't be there in person," Quayle said, "but the
Secret Service wouldn't allow it. I argued that I met with
the Sandinistas in Nicaragua, why not Knight? But their
answer made a lot of sense to me: You can negotiate with
the Sandinistas."

Senator Edward Kennedy's 50th birthday party was actually a political fundraiser for Kennedy's reelection campaign. Among the 200 guests at the $500-a-plate dinner
were actress Lauren Bacall, Jacqueline Onassis, Norman
Mailer, and Lena Horne. "Age," insisted Kennedy, "is really a state of mind."

Willie Nelson celebrated his 50th birthday on tour. According to Willie's bus driver, "Gator" Moore, "We had a
huge ornate birthday cake in the back room of the bus

parked behind the Holiday Inn in Las Vegas. Richard Pryor showed up with his monster bodyguard. Pryor walks in and says, 'Nice cake, Will. It's beautiful.'

"Willie says, 'Why, thank you.'

"Pryor says, 'Happy Birthday.'

"And Pryor went whap! Hurled his whole face and chest headlong into the cake. Buried himself in it.

"So Willie picks up a double armload of cake and mashes it all over Pryor's bodyguard.

" 'A happy birthday to all,' Willie says."

When actor Dennis Hopper turned 50, he was making the film *Texas Chainsaw Massacre Part 2*. The cast and crew threw him a surprise party on the set, wheeling out a huge cake bordered with 50 candles. Then someone handed Hopper a chainsaw to slice the cake. The highlight of Hopper's day, though, came when he took the rest of the day off to play golf with his good friend Willie Nelson.

Earl Browder, the former secretary-general of the American Communist Party, celebrated his 50th birthday party with little fanfare as a prisoner in the federal penitentiary in Atlanta.

● ● ● ● ●

"It doesn't hurt. I don't think it's any great deal. Anyone with a little luck and a penchant for life will reach this most curious age."

—WILLIE MORRIS

"It is more of a milestone than other birthdays, because it brings with it intimations of mortality. I've thought about it more than becoming either thirty or forty, which had practically no impact."

—GLORIA STEINEM

● ● ● ● ●

Gloria Steinem's 50th birthday party was a gala affair, as 750 celebrities gathered at the Waldorf-Astoria in Manhattan to honor Steinem. Guests at the $250-per-plate affair—to raise funds for the Ms. Foundation—included Alan Alda, George McGovern, Ralph Nader (in a frumpy brown suit), Helen Gurley Brown, and Marlo Thomas. Talk-show host Phil Donahue acted as master of ceremonies, and music for the occasion was provided by Kit McClure and her All-Woman Band, with a special appearance by Bette Midler, who capped the evening with a musical tribute to "Great Big Knockers."

● ● ● ● ●

Music for a Fiftieth Birthday:
Albums Made by Rock Stars over 50
(or at least 49)

Off the Ground, Paul McCartney
Wandering Spirit, Mick Jagger
Rhythm of the Saints, Paul Simon
Live, Jerry Garcia Band
Foreign Affair, Tina Turner
Warm Your Heart, Aaron Neville
Time Takes Time, Ringo Starr

Color My Dreams, Carole King
Phobia, The Kinks
Main Offender, Keith Richards
Live in Japan, George Harrison
Hymns to the Silence, Van Morrison
Mystery Girl, Roy Orbison

"Help yourself to *Modern Maturity*; me, I'm signing up for *Jack and Jill* and *My Weekly Reader* and *Seventeen*. Tomorrow I'm getting a skateboard, and next week I'm taking Nintendo classes. I may need six years to grow one, but I aim to have a pigtail down the back of my neck and to learn what a Bon Jovi is; I'd thought it was a cleansing powder, but I think I was wrong."

—JONATHAN YARDLEY

"It was my birthday but I didn't think of it."

—ANDY WARHOL

• • • • •

Andy Warhol's friends threw him a surprise party at the New York home of fashion designer Halston. Singer Lou Reed presented Warhol with a one-inch television, Halston gave him a white fur coat, another gentleman friend gave Andy the shirt off his back and made him put it on, and the evening came to a close when someone filled a garbage can with two thousand one-dollar bills and dumped it on Warhol's head. "It really was the best present," Andy decided.

Elizabeth Taylor celebrated her 50th birthday quietly, with a glass of wine, in her native city of London, where she was starring in a revival of *The Little Foxes.*

Reprinted with permission from Hallmark Cards, Inc.

To mark Bugs Bunny's 50th birthday in 1990, CBS aired a one-hour prime-time all-star television special ("Hollywood Salutes Bugs' Fiftieth Birthday"); Warner Home Video released a limited-edition videocassette featuring clips from Bugs's most memorable cartoons; Six Flags amusement parks sponsored special Bugs-oriented events throughout the summer; an exhibit of vintage animation art featuring Bugs and his friends made a tour of museums across America; and "Box Office Bunny," the first new Bugs Bunny short in twenty-six years, debuted at movie theaters. Bugs, incidentally, is the same age as Raquel Welch.

At his 50th birthday party in February 1975, Paul Newman received a wicker wheelchair filled with presents, and Neil Sedaka sang *The Most Beautiful Man in the World* just for him.

Aretha Franklin celebrated her 50th birthday with 150 friends (including basketball star Isiah Thomas and Levi Stubbs, lead singer of the Four Tops) at her posh mansion in an affluent Detroit suburb. Franklin refused to admit her age, claiming that she was "thirty-five and holding": "Whatever the celebrity registers say, they'll have to check with the soul register, the lady's register. They'll have to check with me." Nevertheless, the Queen of Soul won the *Turning 50* birthday banquet award by treating her guests to a combined gourmet and soul food buffet that included chicken and green onions on a skewer, chitterlings, candied sweet potatoes, filet mignon, shrimp tempura, collard greens, corn on the cob, lobster, shrimp, and rice pudding—and for dessert, a three-layer pound cake with raspberry and lemon cream filling.

On Albert Einstein's 50th birthday, his Berlin apartment was flooded with messages and presents from admirers. The world-renowned physicist's gifts, not all of which actually fit into his flat, included an honorary degree from the University of Paris, a new house from the city of Berlin, a handsome mahogany-finished sailboat (Einstein loved to sail along the nearby Havel River), and an announcement from American Zionists that they planned to acquire land near Jerusalem to plant a grove of trees that would be known as Einstein Forest. Although his wife was at their apartment to fend off inquiries from overzealous journalists, Einstein himself had fled the spotlight for the peace of the Berlin suburbs, where he enjoyed a quiet birthday dinner of stuffed pike and mushrooms.

"When my forty-ninth birthday rolled around, he [husband Allen Ludden] devised an elaborately wonderful surprise party that really worked. Somehow, without my having a clue, he managed to get forty-nine good friends together and marched me into the most complete surprise of my life. In a funny, touching toast, he explained that he was hoping to soften the edge of the Big One coming up next year.

"The upshot, of course, was that when the next year rolled around, he was stuck with another party to celebrate 'The Big One.' "

—BETTY WHITE

Adolf Hitler celebrated his 50th birthday in April 1939. The King of England sent his personal greetings, as did the Pope, and church bells rang as special masses were celebrated "to implore God's blessing upon Fuhrer and people" in swastika-decorated German churches. One Nazi party leader gave Hitler a brand-new Volkswagen, the revolutionary and inexpensive German-made car that had not yet been made available to the public. Gifts from the Fuhrer's grateful subjects filled three rooms of the

Reich Chancellery; among them were six thousand pairs of hand-knitted socks, an assortment of daggers and knives, hand grenades and pistols, a live eagle, and a six-foot birthday cake.

Since Joan Crawford had lied about her age when she arrived in Hollywood, she turned 50 on what she claimed was her 46th birthday. In any event, she refused to have any sort of festivities to mark the occasion. "What's there to celebrate?" asked Crawford, who was drinking vodka day and night at the time. "No. It reminds me that I'm getting older."

"I slept well and developed lots of brand new ideas. You know, I deal in ideas now—I have passed the stage where I have to carry them out."

—VIHJALMUR STEFANSSON

"Really, one should ignore one's fiftieth birthday. As anyone over fifty will tell you, it's no age at all. All the same . . . it's hard not to look back and wonder why one hasn't done more, or forward and wonder what, if anything, one will do in the future."

—PHILIP LARKIN

"I greeted the arrival of my fiftieth birthday this month with uninhibited joy. . . . I proudly wore the button stating 50—THE LEGEND LIVES ON that a good friend gave me to mark the day. I loved hearing younger strangers say incredulously, 'You're fifty?' as if it gave them new respect for and optimism about the prospect of that landmark age."

—JANE BRODY, personal health columnist,
New York Times

Jane Brody's Healthful Dinner for a 50th Birthday Bash

Hummus, Eggplant Spread, and
  Whole Wheat Pita Toasts
Baked Halibut Steaks
  (cooked with herbs but no butter)
Steamed Asparagus
Dilled New Potatoes
Cucumber and Leek Salad
Whole-grain Bread
Carrot Cake with Low-fat Icing
  (and five candles)

Although Elvis Presley had already been dead for nearly seven years, the media revived him long enough to observe what would have been his 50th birthday in January 1985. Home Box Office produced a tribute featuring live footage filmed during Elvis's comeback television special, and RCA allegedly spent more than $500,000 promoting new and recycled releases on commemorative albums and compact disc boxed sets. Then "Blue Suede Shoes" was re-released as a single, pressed on blue vinyl, and a video of the song appeared on MTV.

* * *

Weary of the world, the romantic Italian poet Gabriele D'Annunzio announced at the age of 50 that he had experienced everything life had to offer. He promised to live one more year, then bring his existence to an end in some mysterious and explosive manner, leaving no trace behind.

● ● ● ● ●

"It was very sobering because it became apparent to me that two-thirds of my life was over. It was a time to really take stock of what I wanted to do with the rest of my life."
—CAROLE SIMPSON

Chiang Kai-shek celebrated his 50th birthday in 1936 with a patriotic display designed to encourage his Chinese Nationalist subjects to fight on against the Japanese troops that had invaded the mainland. The occasion was marked by patriotic parades and the appearance in Nanking of inspirational posters showing Chiang, sword in hand, leaping to the top of the Great Wall to lead his countrymen in an assault against the Japanese foe. To emphasize the point, Chiang's colleagues presented him with a birthday cake adorned with fifty models of foreign-built bombers, while fifty real planes were purchased with subscriptions to Chiang's special Birthday Airplane Fund.

> "O, wad me some pawky power
> Gie me a gowden giftie,
> I'd like to stop at forty-nine,
> But pontificate like fifty."
> —OGDEN NASH

Dolly Parton reportedly gave her husband, Carl Dean, what he wanted most for his 50th birthday—"a promise to spend more time with him."

Saddam Hussein waited until his 53rd birthday to stage an Arabian extravaganza. First, he ordered all the top Iraqi government officials to his home village for a two-hour parade in which marchers carried banners that proclaimed, "YOUR CANDLES, SADDAM, ARE THE TORCHES FOR ALL THE ARABS." Then there appeared a primitive cabin—ostensibly a model of Saddam's birthplace—in front of which demonstrators dressed in ancient Babylonian robes prostrated themselves. When the cabin door was opened, fifty-three white doves flew out and up into the sky.

Warren Beatty, on the other hand, celebrated his 53rd birthday by treating his friends to a banquet of El Pollo Loco chicken and Big Macs.

"The day I turned fifty was one of the most rewarding and happiest days of my life. Three hundred of my friends flew in from around the world for my birthday party. I felt like I was 19."

—WILMA RUDOLPH

Sigmund Freud shares the *Turning 50* award for the weirdest birthday celebration. To honor the father of psychotherapy, a group of his Viennese admirers presented Freud with a special medallion: one side showed his profile in bas-relief, and on the other there was a scene of Oedipus answering the sphinx, accompanied by an inscription from Sophocles: "Who divined the famed riddle and was a man most mighty." When he read these words, Freud turned deathly pale and demanded to know who had thought of putting the quotation on the coin. He later confided that years before, while he was a student at the university in Vienna, he had imagined seeing his own bust on the grounds, bearing precisely the same inscription.

> *"Fifty today, old lad?*
> *Well, that's not doing so bad . . .*
> *The next fifty won't be so good,*
> *True, but for now—touch wood—*
> *You can eat and booze and the rest of it,*
> *Still get a lot of the best of it."*
>
> —KINGSLEY AMIS

Not surprisingly, Shirley MacLaine shares with Freud *Turning 50*'s award for the most bizarre birthday party. The night before she turned 50, MacLaine's friends rented a New York City disco and decorated it entirely in white—white lilies, white roses, white balloons, white silk on the walls—and hung crystals from the eight-foot-high floral arrangements. It was all designed to re-create what MacLaine referred to as "a Love and Light temple out of one of my old Atlantean lifetimes." To match this spiritual theme, all the guests (including Liberace) were required to wear white; those who did not own white suits arrived in sheets or jogging outfits. Dinner consisted of white asparagus, assorted health foods, and a birthday carrot cake.

But that was merely the pre-birthday party. On the day

Shirley actually turned 50, the producer of her Broadway show rented an elephant from the circus and presented it to Shirley so she could take a pachyderm ride up Fifth Avenue. She claimed she enjoyed the experience tremendously.

MOVIES FOR A
50th
BIRTHDAY

The Lion in Winter (1968)—Peter O'Toole and Katharine Hepburn as King Henry II of England and Eleanor of Aquitaine, each closing in on 50, and neither one giving an inch to age or the younger generation. Favorite line: Hepburn saying, "If you break, it's because you're brittle." One of the greatest movies made during the last fifty years.

The Wild Bunch (1969)—The over-the-hill gang rides one more time. Featuring aging outlaws William Holden, Ernest Borgnine, Robert Ryan, Warren Oates, and Ben Johnson. "I was trying to tell a simple story about bad men in changing times," explained director Sam Peckinpah. "The strange thing is that you feel a great sense of loss when these killers reach the end of the line."

A superlative film with veteran actors who know what the hell they're doing.

Fifty–Fifty (1986)—A pleasant little Canadian film. Unfortunately, if you look for it at your local video rental store, your chances of finding it are considerably less than 50–50.

High Noon (1952)—Gary Cooper was 50 years old when he made this classic western, and was suffering the entire time from stomach ulcers and a painful hip injury. Nevertheless, Cooper proved just how much honest emotion—including a healthy measure of fear—could be conveyed with a face that had seen a half-century.

Best Friends (1983)—A made-for-television movie that opens with Elizabeth Taylor's character celebrating her 50th birthday, dancing drunkenly atop a coffee table. It gets better as Taylor's friend, another 50-year-old played by Carol Burnett, refuses to let her succumb to self-pity.

Never Say Never Again (1983)—Sean Connery as James Bond at the age of 53, back after a twelve-year hiatus to battle villain Klaus Maria Brandauer. Barbara Carrera makes it all worthwhile.

The Guns of Navarone (1961)—A highly improbable but hugely entertaining saga of middle-aged commandos sabotaging a German gun emplacement during World War II. David Niven was 50 years old when he made this film; Anthony Quayle was 48, and Gregory Peck and Anthony Quinn were 45.

All About Eve (1950)—Bette Davis in Hollywood's version of what happens to actresses as they close in on 50. Compare this to such virile masculine epics as *High Noon* and *The Guns of Navarone*.

Whatever Happened to Baby Jane? (1962)—Bette Davis again as an aging movie star, this time with Joan Crawford.

Slap Shot (1977)—Paul Newman pretending to be an aging hockey player in his late forties.

Lonely Hearts (1981)—An Australian charmer about romance in middle age, between a shy office worker and a piano tuner. Lovely performances.

Will Penny (1968)—Charlton Heston as a cowboy and a loner—"dirty, ignorant, not overly courageous, and fifty years old." Critical reviews were mixed, but it remains a powerful tale of survival and self-reliance.

Sea of Love (1990)—Al Pacino as a middle-aged undercover cop who passes himself off as former New York

Yankee shortstop Phil Rizzuto to catch some crooks. Pacino obviously had mellowed by the time he hit 50; he never would have joked about his height when he was younger.

Eighteen Again! (1982)—Dream on.

INTERVIEW WITH
TOM PETERS

Tom Peters, one of the nation's leading business management gurus, recently wrote a column on "What I've Learned At 50" (see below). Tom's basic philosophy, both in life and business, is that we must remain open to new opportunities, to pursuing unexpected avenues for growth when they appear, and refuse to be locked into dull routine, even by success. Between his frequent speaking engagements, I caught up with Tom and asked him to elaborate on his thoughts.

Q: You turned fifty last November (1992). Did you take that occasion to pause and take stock of where you were?

A: Not in the way that some people do. I know that some people make a big symbolic deal out of the birthday *per se*, which is fine and dandy. That just doesn't happen to fit my style. But I would certainly say that the upcom-

ing nature of the fiftieth birthday—for many months before, and subsequently many months afterward, to this
day—has been, in the longer sense of the word, a real
prod to thinking a little more seriously about life than one
normally does when you're caught up in your regular
routine.

Q: I guess that's true. It *is* a half-century.

A: That's right. Exactly. (Laughs.) It's a half-century
and, unless you're one hell of an optimist, you're not on
the upside of the curve.

Q: Do you feel different, having turned fifty?

A: Well, no, certainly in the sense of physiological differences. That process of aging goes on slowly, starting I
think at the age of twenty, or something like that. But I do
feel different, at least for me—and obviously all this stuff
is completely different on an individual basis—in the real
sense that if you're not doing the sorts of things that you
want to be doing, then you really ought to be watching
yourself at this stage of the game.

When a guy like Ross Perot—forget the presidency
run—when Perot sells EDS to General Motors and then, a
couple of years later at age sixty-one or sixty-two, opens
up a giant new company like Perot Systems, I'm always
amazed by that. This drive for achievement that an awful
lot of us have—it seems to me at times that it's not a matter of failing to sniff the roses. It's a matter of failing to
take a look at some of the broader opportunities that can
be yours.

I'm not much for the time-management kinds of books,
but I remember years ago coming across one little piece in
a time-management book where a guy said, "If you've just

been diagnosed as having a mortal illness and you've got six months to live, if you would change your priorities dramatically from what you're doing today, then today is the time to change from what you're doing without getting the diagnosis."

So certainly the fiftieth birthday, much more than forty for me, is the time to think about that. Forty was just another step along the way. This is a totally different ball game.

Q: I think that's true. You really do get more of a sense of impending mortality, I suppose, at fifty.

A: Yes. You know, the other side of that for people who are climbing up the rungs of a company, and these big companies in particular, where the senior leadership positions often don't come until you're fifty—a lot of them are just catching their first steam, or something like that. And that's amazing to me.

Q: If you think back to when you were twenty-five, are you now where you thought you'd be when you hit fifty?

A: Oh, no. No. I had no more idea of where I was going to be at twenty-six, let alone forty-six or fifty. It's all been a great mysterious and amazing process to me, both the ups and the downs along the way.

Q: Do you have any idea where you'll be in another twenty or twenty-five years?

A: Absolutely not. Not only do I not have an idea, but I don't want to have an idea. I find nothing more appalling—again, all of this is completely personal, and I have great admiration for people who have views that are totally the opposite of my own—but the thought of having a life planned for me is beneath contempt.

Q: And yet there are people like that.
A: Absolutely. There are people I know who have five hundred drawers for individual pairs of socks.

Q: When I spoke with Jerry Greenfield (of Ben and Jerry's Ice Cream) about turning forty, his main complaint was that his stomach wouldn't hold as much, and that he couldn't eat as much ice cream as he used to.
A: Yeah, that's a professional problem for him. I certainly agree with that in the larger sense of things. A third glass of wine sends me around the bend these days. When I was a youngster that was not the case at all. Whether it's food or booze or whatever, you certainly become increasingly aware of your limits, and that's an understatement.

Q: Nothing else comes to mind along that line?
A: No. The nice part for me is almost the opposite of that. I took up obsessive exercising only about five years ago, and by a lot of measures I'm in better shape at the age of fifty than I have been since I was playing college athletics at the age of twenty. I can do stuff at fifty that I couldn't do at forty, and that's literally the truth.

Q: You mentioned in your column that "success begets failure," that we continue to do the same things that have brought us rewards, and eventually we fall into a rut. How do you get around that?
A: It's damn near impossible. Unfortunately, I think all of us respond to applause, and when you do something well, all sorts of pressures are in place to keep doing it. It's

something that troubles me professionally, as well as personally, because I see it in companies all the time as well, which is mostly of course what I worry about for a living. When companies are successful, they just turn up the heat under whatever they've done in the past, and eventually the world catches up with them.

One of the tricks that I have not learned, and am in desperate pursuit of, is how to make that major shift of gears to go after something entirely new, which I think is good for the soul and good for the spirit. But when the applause keeps coming, it's darned difficult to go from being the world's expert in whatever to beginning all over again.

When I look at most of the things that have happened to me in my life, they've happened because of something I had not intended, something that came out of the blue, that forced me to dramatically change my direction.

One of the things I'm aware of is the difference between the age of fifteen and the age of fifty, in that you are more intimidated by learning new things. At the age of fifty, and maybe even before that, taking up a totally new sport, or learning how to do anything new of significance—our grooves do get deeper as time goes on.

Q: Have you noticed that your outlook has changed as you neared fifty, in terms of what is important in your life?

A: Yes, definitely. There's no question that I pay an awful lot more attention to all of life and important personal relationships as opposed to the sort of business-professional trajectory that traditionally has driven the male. And I notice that significantly.

My wife and I, about four or five years ago, decided to

split our time between Vermont and California, and so we ended up in a very different setting—Vermont—with a very different metabolism than the one we'd been in before. Hanging out on a farm for six months a year gives you a greater appreciation of what goes on in the world than hanging out in a madcap area like Silicon Valley.

Q: Do you have any words of wisdom for people who are about to turn fifty?

A: Well, the real answer to that is yes, I do, but I don't trust them. These words of wisdom are words of wisdom being directed from me to me. But to my mind, the key is that at fifty, thanks to medical advances and other things, you are relatively young. With any luck at all, you have fifteen or twenty *energetic* years left, which is something we couldn't say years ago. And it is the ideal time to broaden your interests, start a second career—not meaning necessarily something that has to do with eight-to-five work—but really to follow a new passion, and become engaged more broadly in the world. To my mind, that's the key. I'm trying to do something and shift away rather dramatically in the next couple of years, and at least part of me will be very disappointed if I don't manage to pull that off. I'm terrified above all of the rut of continuing to do what you're doing simply because you've done it in the past. The world is such a fantastic and rich place. There's never been a better time to reinvent yourself, and you've got a lot of very energetic time ahead of you.

Tom Peters's List of Things
He Has Learned at 50

1. Unintended consequences outnumber intended consequences.
2. Certainty is a delusion.
3. Fiction beats nonfiction. ("Only the best fiction conveys the richness of life.")
4. Success begets failures. (See interview, above.)
5. Democracy and markets are untidy, but effective.
6. Try it.
7. Vermont farmers have a lot to teach us.
8. Lighten up.
9. Neckties are diabolical. (Amen.)
10. Smile if it kills you.
11. Each day is a miracle.
12. Beware true believers.
13. Reject simple explanations. ("There are no answers. Just, at best, a few guesses that might be worth a try.")

THE 50s
IN HOLLYWOOD

There is an old joke in Hollywood that runs something like this: To find the age of an actress, take the year of her birth, subtract it from itself, and then burn the paper the figures were written on. Then add the number of letters received in last week's fan mail to the box-office receipts from the actress's last film, subtract her salary, divide the remainder by the number of press agents she employs, subtract the number of times she's been married, and knock off ten years on general principles. Then, if the age is still higher than the one the producer wants, figure in mathematical errors until the figure comes out right.

Okay, this sounds silly, but the fact remains that Hollywood producers (and perhaps moviegoers as well) treat 50-year-old actresses differently from their male counterparts. For instance, only 9 percent of the film roles in 1992 went to women over 40. Clint Eastwood at 50, or even 60, is still considered a sex symbol. But Cher at 50—well, I suppose there are better examples. Perhaps the difference is all in our perceptions. Look through the following observations and see what I mean.

"By the time we hit fifty, we have learned our hardest lessons. We have found out that only a few things are really important. We have learned to take life seriously, but never ourselves."

—MARIE DRESSLER

"If a woman of fifty is very thin, she can pass for years younger."

—AUDREY HEPBURN

"I wouldn't mind being called middle-aged if only I knew a few more one-hundred-year-old people."

—DEAN MARTIN AT 50

"I thought I'd be dead before I was thirty. Turning forty stunned me. Fifty is a major miracle, and I think I may even make seventy."

—DENNIS HOPPER

"I want to be leading-man age. I think I'll be gorgeous at fifty. I think that's a nice age for men—and for women."

—WOODY ALLEN

"Half a century. It is the only birthday that has ever meant anything to me at all. But midsummer, in Ireland, up it popped. I suddenly thought, I'm half a century and what haven't I done? What is there to do? I'd done an awful lot. Maybe not the right things. For the first time I became contemplative. It was quite astounding."

—PETER O'TOOLE

"The older I get, the luckier I am."

—NATALIE WOOD

"As a woman, I don't fear age at all, not even fifty. Why should I worry about being fifty? I would have had the man I wanted, I swear I would have had him. I would have had the kind of life I wanted. And if I weren't afraid of death I would be delighted to be fifty."

—MELINA MERCOURI

"There's a difference. Before, the girls would come up to me and say, 'Can I have an autograph?' Now the girls ask for an autograph, and they add, 'It's for my mother.'"

—OMAR SHARIF

"I've only had two experiences during my fifty years. One with Joanne [Woodward], the other with Redford."

—PAUL NEWMAN

"It wasn't a question of whether I'm now going to play 'age.' It was a fact of not trying to do anything about what I am. [pretending to be a fan] 'Ah, he's an old guy now! He's getting wrinkled! Look at the lines in his face.' "

—ROBERT REDFORD

"I make my own decisions now. I've learned that if I make a wrong choice, the world doesn't end, it just goes right on. I'm still shy, but I'm not aloof any longer. I like the person I've become."

—MARY TYLER MOORE

"Since I turned forty, women have liked me a lot better. Up until then, most women who saw me on screen hated my guts. Now that I'm getting a little long in the tooth, they like me to look good."

—RAQUEL WELCH AT 47

"Maybe it's partly that I'm fifty-three years old, and I've come to realize that if I'm going to do anything for the causes I believe in, I've got to do it now."

—ED ASNER

"I think it's terrific to be fifty. Today I'm a building with a basement. It's taken me this long to learn where all the faucets are, to realize I have some pretty solid plumbing—even a nice hot boiler! With that basement, the Rita building can't crumble. At twenty I didn't even feel I had a ground floor."

—RITA MORENO

50!
The first 50 years are the hardest, they say ...
... so kick up your heels 'cause the fun starts today!
Hope your SECOND half-century is terrific!

"The truth of the matter is, I feel pretty strange to be dating at my age. When I grew up, women in their fifties were generally grandmothers who stayed at home with their husbands and were visited by their children and grandchildren. They weren't running about town with a variety of men. Well, I've had to rethink my views, and believe me, I'm not alone."

—ELIZABETH TAYLOR

"You shouldn't drag yourself down because you turn fifty! If you have achieved something in life, age doesn't scare you."

—SOPHIA LOREN

"I don't want to be hip anymore. . . . I always thought that was important. I'm in the slow-learner department. Some of us are slower than others. It's really a symptom of the disease called I'm-only-somebody-if-you're-looking-at-me."

—ALI MACGRAW AT 52

"I am fifty-two and I look it. . . . I am middle-aged and not ashamed of it. It is not something you catch, like a disease. It is not the flu. If a woman has been filled with life, with joy and love and tears, then waking up suddenly at middle age can be a wonderful experience."

—SIMONE SIGNORET

"I turned fifty this year."

"How was it?"

"No f—ing good. I didn't like it."

—JACK NICHOLSON

"I just do my job like everybody else. If a certain appeal works for you, whether it's somebody you've developed over the years or were fortunate enough to have been born with, you don't sit around and analyze it. If you did, you wouldn't have it."

—CLINT EASTWOOD

"I'm not as macho as several years before. In the old days I was very driven. Now I'm striving hard to control compulsive tendencies."

—JANE FONDA

"They used to shoot Shirley Temple through gauze. They ought to shoot me through linoleum."

—TALLULAH BANKHEAD AT 54

"I had fame and fortune as a young man, and now, at fifty-seven, I wouldn't want to be that young again for anything in the world. I loved turning fifty—it meant I was a true survivor, as an actor and as a human being. I'm not looking for a fountain of youth, as some actors are. Some of them, poor things, are constantly trying to look and act young, young, young. Instead, they wind up immature."

—SEAN CONNERY

"By the time you reach fifty, and you begin to see the final curtain and realize that today is not forever, you'd better have reconciled your excesses or you're dead already."

—TONY CURTIS

"Perhaps women enjoy watching other women aging. It's certainly much tougher on a woman to wrinkle and crumble. A man, no matter how old he gets, can always wear an ascot tie and toupee and pretend he's Fred Astaire."

—GROUCHO MARX

"As the years go on, you see changes in yourself, but you've got to face that—everyone goes through it. I can't be a leading lady all my life. That's why I'd be thrilled if people offered me character parts in the future. I won't resent it. Either you have to face up to it and tell yourself you're not going to be eighteen all your life, or be prepared for a terrible shock when you see the wrinkles and white hair."

—AUDREY HEPBURN AT 50

"I've got the kind of metabolism that's going to hold up well against the ravages of time. Too much emphasis is placed on chronological age. I would rather be older and look younger than be younger and look older. I think of myself as a woman of thirty-five."

—JOAN COLLINS AT 50

"I'm fifty years old and I want to look like Jackie Cooper's grandson."

—JOHN BARRYMORE

"It's hard to conceive of myself at this age. I was always the sixteen-year-old prodigy."

—WOODY ALLEN AT 54

"I feel exactly the same as I've always felt: a lightly reined-in voracious beast."

—JACK NICHOLSON AT 55

"Fifty-two is what I am, and I can't look back and find another age that I like better because I wasn't as happy. One lesson I had to learn was to be less available to other people and their needs and more aware of my own."

—POLLY BERGEN

"I finally realize that it's okay to make commercial films and not to worry about each one being a big hit. My life doesn't *depend* on it. . . .

"What the hell? If I fall off the wire, I know now that I'll bounce off the safety net. I'm out of the tunnel and can see the mountain. That's why I try to get up and say, 'What about today? What am I going to do *today*?' "

—AL PACINO

"I'm a little more serious. Life isn't a throwaway anymore."

—BILLY DEE WILLIAMS

"A woman really hits her peak between fifty and fifty-
five. A man is attractive at fifty-five to sixty, maybe until
sixty-two."

—WOODY ALLEN

"I admit that today the 'new' Elizabeth Taylor is my greatest role. At fifty-five years old, by golly, I've become a sex
symbol again."

—ELIZABETH TAYLOR

"The secret is that I don't act my age. My kids have an
eleven-year-old mom."

—CAROL BURNETT

"We're just the same age, Montand and I. He's lived beside me while I aged, and I've lived beside him while he
matured. That's one of the differences between men and
women. They mature; their white hair is called 'silvery
temples,' the lines on their faces are 'chiseled,' and sometimes they trot their fifties around."

—SIMONE SIGNORET

"In the end, an actress has only two ways to go: quit at the
top, like Garbo, or shift into character parts, as I did. Ac-

tors go on playing romantic leads with a new crop of star-
lets; actresses are relegated to doting mothers, fluttering
aunties, or monsters."

—MYRNA LOY

"Look at Katharine Hepburn. Look at Bette Davis. Some
of Hollywood's great actresses came into their primes in
their middle forties because you're better at your work if
you let it happen and do not fight the passage of time."

—SHIRLEY MACLAINE

"This can be the time in a woman's life that is tragic. You
can either kill yourself ultimately, or you can fade away
into some small community around for us movie stars,
like Santa Barbara. What I'd like, I suppose, is to die with
my boots on."

—FAYE DUNAWAY

"There comes a time when you've simply got to face the
fact that you're an old broad. And I have. I'm not scared
of growing old. Not at all. I'll never be one of those
women who looks in the mirror and weeps."

—AVA GARDNER

"Who cares, anyway?"

—NICOL WILLIAMSON, on being confronted
with evidence that he was
52 years old, not 49

LIFE BEGINS AT 50

(PERHAPS)

Back in 1932, a Columbia University professor named Walter B. Pitkin wrote a thin volume called *Life Begins at Forty*, in which he explained that people who reached that milestone in the modern era were—unlike their ancestors—blessed with the chance to spend the rest of their lives enjoying their leisure time, simplifying their lives, and concentrating on a few powerful, enduring wishes.

In the nineties, however, this sort of relaxed outlook on life seems to kick in at 50 rather than 40. By the time you turn 50, psychologists tell us, you have discovered who you are and what your priorities are. As Carl Jung pointed out, these are the years when people begin to "make up their souls," striving to consolidate their experience into a fuller knowledge of the world and mankind.

Even the dreaded midlife crisis has been pushed back at

least a decade. After all, Dante was only 35 when he suffered the first recorded instance of a midlife crisis: "Mid-
way life's journey," the Italian poet wrote, "I was made
aware that I had strayed into a dark forest, and the right
path appeared not anywhere." A prominent Beverly Hills
psychologist who specializes in this overrated phenomenon claims that her patients, who used to suffer attacks of
anxiety between the ages of 35 and 45, now tend to fall
apart between 45 and 55 instead. A comforting notion indeed, especially with a president in his mid-forties in the
White House.

In a number of non–Western cultures, the advent of
middle age actually provides individuals with a new lease
on life. The change is particularly marked for women,
who no longer have to focus their energies on raising a
family. Now *they* are the matriarchs who govern the
household, arranging marriages and ordering the lives of
their daughters-in-law. Indeed, in many societies—
including our own—women and men tend to cross paths
after 50, as men become more nurturing and family-
oriented, while women often become more aggressive and
independent. Jung described this as a "contrasexual transition," but it may simply stem from all of us growing
weary of the roles we have been playing for most of our
adult lives, and longing for the rewards enjoyed by the
opposite sex.

It is, perhaps, no accident that Digger Phelps retired as
head coach of the Notre Dame basketball team at the age
of 49, or that Joe Gibbs resigned as the Washington Red-
skins' coach at 51 to pursue other interests (including
race-car driving). In that spirit, we can celebrate those
who decided to start a new life around age 50, as well as
the grouches who decided to pack it all in.

● ● ● ● ●

"A man's beginning his prime at fifty, or there never was much man in him."

—George Meredith

"Having begun work so young, I felt that at fifty it was due me to have freedom from absorption in active business affairs, and to devote myself to a variety of interests other than money making, which had claimed a portion of my time since the beginning of my business career."

—John D. Rockefeller

"There is only so much time in the game of life. Between the ages of fifty and sixty, I better attempt the other challenges because things change between sixty and seventy."

—Richard "Digger" Phelps, on his retirement as Notre Dame basketball coach at 49

"As many a too industrious millionaire has discovered, one cannot learn to idle at the age of fifty."

—Robert Lynd

"A midlife crisis is a lot like the Army, only the food is better."

—Gerald Nadiman

"A young man's ambition is to get along in the world and make a place for himself—half your life goes that way, till you're forty-five or fifty. Then, if you're lucky, you make terms with life, you get released."

—ROBERT PENN WARREN

"At age fifty I can start something new—I can go live on a beach and work in a card shop. I can try to direct movies if that's what I want to do. I can take chances then."

—LINDA ELLERBEE

"Between forty-five and fifty-five, I take it, is when a man ought to do the work into which he expects to put most of himself."

—WOODROW WILSON

"From forty to fifty a man must move upward, or the natural falling off in the vigor of life will carry him rapidly downward."

—OLIVER WENDELL HOLMES, JR.

● ● ● ● ●

At the age of 50, Henry Adams yearned to return to the South Seas (from where he had recently returned), "if it were only to sleep forever in the trade-winds under the southern stars, wandering over the dark purple ocean, with its purple sense of solitude and void."

When Henry Ford turned 50, he still was not listed in *Who's Who*, even though he was probably making more money per year than anyone else in the United States. It was during his 50th year that Ford instituted the assembly-line production techniques that revolutionized American industry.

"Today, I accept the inevitable more serenely. I know that I will never write as many books as Georges Simenon or read as many as Edmund Wilson. Nor will I enter a game in late September to triple up the alley in center field and win a pennant for the Mets. But my daughters live on their own in the world. I have read much of Henry James and the best of Balzac and have walked the marbled acres of the Pitti Palace. Middle age is part of the process of completion of a life, and that is why I've come to lose the fear of death."

—PETE HAMILL

"At fifty, you begin to examine the passbook of your life with a new urgency. Suddenly, all those casual promissory notes of years gone by are overdue. Oh, migod, I still haven't learned French. Or chess. Or whatever."

—TOM BROKAW

"A world in which people may reorient their whole lives at forty or fifty is a world in which marriage for life becomes more and more difficult. Each spouse is given the right to and the means for growth. Either may discover a hidden talent and begin to develop it, or repudiate a paralyzing neurotic trend and begin anew. Ever since women have been educated, marriages have been endangered by the possible development or failure to develop of both husbands and wives."

—Margaret Mead

Paul Newman took up race-car driving at the age of 47. "I didn't do it to prove anything," Newman explained. "It wasn't a matter of courage. It was simply a confirmation of whimsicality and irresponsibility."

"Just why Lincoln took to whiskers at this time [at the age of 52] nobody seemed to know. A girl in New York State had begged him to raise a beard. But something more than her random wish guided him. Herndon, Whitney, Lamon, Nicolay, Hay heard no explanation from him as to why after fifty-two years with a smooth face he should now change."

—Carl Sandburg

"The general, besides, was in the prime of life—that is, fifty-six, and not a day older, which under any circumstances is the most flourishing age in a man's life, the age at which *real* life can be rightly said to begin."

—Fyodor Dostoyevsky

"Now we know what the young find hard to believe— that you can always break the rules so long as you know what they are. We may not be able to beat them in a long run, but we have mapped all the shortcuts."

—ALAN BRIEN

"But now that I am forty-nine, I'm tolerant, and like it fine."

—OGDEN NASH

"It's only in your twenties and in your seventies and eighties that you do the greatest work. The enemy of society is the middle class, and the enemy of life is middle age."

—ORSON WELLES

"In all honesty, so what if I never made another movie again? I'm already fifty; nobody's gonna say I failed."

—JACK NICHOLSON

"At fifty, we should know who we are. We should compare ourselves—a niggling occupation—less frequently with others, having learned to live quietly with our success or failure. It is then that the real competition begins, not with the rival across the street but with the rival inside ourselves."

—CLIFTON FADIMAN

"At past fifty, Adams solemnly and painfully learned to ride the bicycle."

—HENRY ADAMS

FAMOUS AFTER 50

Charles Darwin—Published *On the Origin of Species* at the age of 50.

Winston Churchill—Appointed Chancellor of the Exchequer in 1924, several weeks after his 50th birthday. Not until he was 65, in 1939, did Churchill become prime minister of Great Britain.

Julia Child—Began eating French food at the age of 37, and started her television career as the nation's favorite French chef after she turned 50.

Josef Stalin—Attained supreme power as dictator of the Soviet Union at 50.

Adam Smith—Published *The Wealth of Nations,* the classic text of mercantilism, at 51.

Confucius—At 51, left private life as a tutor to become prime minister of the state of Lu.

Abraham Lincoln—An unsuccessful one-term congressman whose only claim to fame came from his speeches in a losing bid for a seat in the U.S. Senate at the age of 48. Won the presidential election of 1860 at 51.

Gail Borden—Invented condensed milk at 51, allowing him to leave behind his job as a surveyor.

Samuel Morse—Sent the first message via electric telegraph ("What hath God wrought?") at 52.

Edward Gibbon—Finished his masterpiece, *The Decline and Fall of the Roman Empire,* at 52.

Margaret Thatcher—At 53, became the first female prime minister of Great Britain.

Alfred Kinsey—Published his seminal study, *Sexual Behavior of the Human Male,* at 54.

Robert E. Lee—Commanded the Confederate Army of Northern Virginia at 55.

Rachel Carson—At 55, completed *The Silent Spring,* the book that went far toward starting the environmentalist revolution.

Paul Cézanne—Did not have his first solo show until the age of 56.

Miguel de Cervantes—Employed as a commissary officer in the Spanish Royal Navy, until he wrote *Don Quixote* at 59.

P. T. Barnum—A two-bit showman until his "Greatest Show on Earth" opened when he was 61.

WHERE WERE THEY AT 50?

Muhammad Ali—Living on a horse farm in Berrien Springs, Michigan, with his fourth wife.

Benedict Arnold—A merchant and land speculator living in New Brunswick, Canada, obsessed with his reputation as a traitor.

Marcus Aurelius—Emperor of Rome, leading a military campaign against barbarian troops in southern Germany.

Lucille Ball—Divorced from Desi Arnaz and planning to remarry. Launched her second television series, *The Lucy Show*, later that same year.

Bernard Baruch—A multimillionaire from his operations in the stock market.

Judge Roy Bean—A trader, cattle rustler, gambler, and saloonkeeper. At 57, he named himself judge and set up court in his saloon.

Billy the Kid—Dead at 21.

Napoleon Bonaparte—Confined to the island of St. Helena, in exile, following his unsuccessful return to the European continent in 1815.

Michelangelo Buonarotti—Stuck in the middle of an artistic lull that had begun when he turned 40. He eventually revived at 55 and completed one of his greatest masterpieces, the Medici Chapel.

John Chapman (Johnny Appleseed)—Wandering through the wilderness of Ohio and Indiana, planting apple seeds.

Christopher Columbus—Back in Spain, preparing to make his fourth and final voyage to the Americas.

Davy Crockett—Fighting at the Alamo.

Oliver Cromwell—Signed the death warrant of King Charles I of England and was subsequently named Lord Protector.

George Armstrong Custer—Dead at the age of 37. (Well, it was pretty much his own fault.)

Charles de Gaulle—Recently promoted to the rank of general, de Gaulle fled France after the Nazi conquest and became the leader of the Free French opposition based in northern Africa.

Bob Dylan—On the road in South America, with the Never-Ending Tour.

Millard Fillmore—Succeeded to the presidency following the death of Zachary Taylor.

Geronimo—An Apache warrior, leading a campaign of armed resistance to the United States Army's attempts to restrict his people to a reservation in Arizona.

Ulysses S. Grant—Completing his first term as president, preparing to run for a second scandal-filled term in the White House.

Thomas E. Lawrence (Lawrence of Arabia)—Dead at the age of 47.

Benito Mussolini—In his tenth year as dictator of Italy.

Richard Milhous Nixon—Still licking his wounds after his defeat the year before in an election for governor of California.

Juan Ponce de León—Governor of Puerto Rico, about to embark on a search for the Fountain of Youth.

Sir Walter Raleigh—Lodged in the Tower of London, under sentence of death on a trumped-up charge of treason.

Will Rogers—Writing a column for the *New York Times* and starring in his own occasional traveling shows.

William Shakespeare—Retired from writing and producing drama at the age of 49, and retired to his estate at Stratford. He died at 52.

Belle Starr—Leading a band of cattle rustlers and horse thieves, raiding the Oklahoma Territory.

Josip Broz Tito—Leading a band of partisan guerrillas in the mountains of Yugoslavia.

Harry S. Truman—Elected to his first term in the United States Senate.

George Washington—Still in command of the Continental Army, awaiting the successful end of the American Revolution one year later.

PEOPLE WHO,
IF YOU ARE
50,
YOU HAVE ALREADY LIVED
LONGER THAN

Died at age:

Charles Baudelaire—46
Anne Boleyn—29
Cesare Borgia—31
Jim Bowie—40
Charlotte Brontë—39
Robert Burns—37
Albert Camus—47
Enrico Caruso—45
Frédéric Chopin—39
Lord Randolph Churchill—45
Stephen Crane—29
Crazy Horse—28
Stephen A. Douglas—48
F. Scott Fitzgerald—44

Vincent van Gogh—37
Alexander Hamilton—49
O. Henry—48
Wild Bill Hickok—39
John Henry "Doc" Holliday—36
Thomas "Stonewall" Jackson—39
John Paul Jones—45
Janis Joplin—27
Franz Kafka—41
Robert F. Kennedy—43
Ring Lardner—48
D. H. Lawrence—45
Jack London—40
Huey Long—42
Joseph McCarthy—49
Malcolm X—40
Lorenzo de' Medici—43
Jim Morrison—28
George "Baby Face" Nelson—26
George Orwell—47
Richard I (The Lionheart) of England—42
Maximilien Robespierre—36
Rudolph Valentino—31
Oscar Wilde—45
Emiliano Zapata—40

LOVE AND SEX AT 50

Recently I overheard a conversation between four middle-aged women who were discussing whether the chocolate-laden dessert they were eating was better than sex. They all agreed the dessert was marvelous, but in the end they had to leave the question unresolved, since none of them could remember back far enough to make a valid comparison.

Actually, sex and love at 50 are far more common (and enjoyable) than stand-up comics and blockheaded television advertisers might suggest. Certainly there are no shortages of examples among celebrities and famous historical personalities. Humphrey Bogart was nearly 50 when he met Lauren Bacall—then 19 years old—on the set of *To Have and Have Not*. They were wed the following year, and remained happily married until his death in 1957. The French philosopher Voltaire was 50 when he be-

came the fervent lover of his niece, Madame Denis, soon
after her husband died. According to contemporary reports, Madame Denis was quite fat and florid, but that
only seemed to enhance her sex appeal, at least for
Voltaire. Times change.

But time changes more for men than for women. Research studies have proven conclusively that, in the words
of Masters and Johnson, "There is no time limit drawn by
the advancing years to female sexuality." The combination
of more leisure time and privacy (once the kids are grown
and gone) and the dwindling fear of pregnancy enhances
sexual satisfaction—and increases sexual aggressiveness—
among women who have turned 50. Although many
women reach a peak of maximum responsiveness in their
late twenties, they maintain that level for most of the rest
of their lives.

Fifty-year-old men, on the other hand, already have lost
a considerable measure of both desire and capacity. Research by the Kinsey Institute has found that men after 50
"think less about sex and have fewer sexual fantasies than
when they were younger." Hmmm. The average American
male, who experiences 104 orgasms per year (nearly half
of them solo) at the age of 20, is down to 52 orgasms per
year (only 2 solo) by the time he turns 50. What that
means, though, is that actual instances of lovemaking with
a partner are virtually the same at 50 as at 20. The main
difference appears to be that 50-year-old men are less eas-
ily aroused by purely visual stimuli, and everything simply seems to take just a bit longer.

Some men fight the trend by venturing outside the
bonds of marriage. For instance, a recent poll by the National Opinion Research Center reports that 24.3 percent
of men aged 50 to 59 admitted to at least one instance of

infidelity, compared to only 3.3 percent of women in the same age bracket.

And there are, of course, extreme cases of middle-aged men trying to recapture their lost youth through liaisons with high school cheerleaders or nubile college students, though this sort of thing is clearly the exception. Former Rolling Stones bass player Bill Wyman, for instance, married his girlfriend, Mandy Smith, when he was 46 and she was 19. Actually, Wyman had met and fallen in love with Mandy when she was just 15. "I've got bloody goose pimples, like a kid with a new toy," Wyman reportedly gushed. "It's like Christmas and I can't wait to see her again." During their romance, Wyman was jocularly referred to in the press as "the wrinkly Lothario." Not surprisingly, the infatuation did not last. After eighteen months, Wyman and Mandy were divorced.

But the story has a happy ending, of sorts. In April 1993, Wyman got married again, this time to a mature 33-year-old woman. Meanwhile, his son, who was then 30, announced his engagement to Mandy's 46-year-old mother, Patty Smith. Their wedding, if it ever occurs, would eventually make Wyman his ex-wife's stepgrandfather.

● ● ● ● ●

"I think it's only after fifty that a woman becomes truly passionate. At that point, women abdicate certain aspects of their personalties, leave seduction behind. And when seduction is left behind, there is so much more energy, so much more passion."

—GERARD DEPARDIEU

"In my twenties, I didn't have a clue as to what men needed in life. When you get a little older, you are more aware of men's needs, and this is extremely sexy."

—HELEN GURLEY BROWN

"I decided when I turned fifty that I was going to have a pair of knockers, because I lived fifty years without them, putting pads in, taking pads out, and I thought, 'I'm sick and tired of this.'"

—JULIET PROWSE

"For certain people, after fifty, litigation takes the place of sex."

—GORE VIDAL

"From birth to age eighteen, a girl needs good parents. From eighteen to thirty-five, she needs good looks. From thirty-five to fifty-five, she needs a good personality. From fifty-five on, she needs good cash."

—SOPHIE TUCKER

"Fifty is what forty used to be. The frontier of sexuality is being pushed back, too. From Angie Dickinson to Cicely Tyson . . . women who already have passed or are about to reach fifty are remaining whole and sexual people in the public eye."

—GLORIA STEINEM

"Not that I'm in the market, but for an older woman to be interested in me she'd have to be sixty."

—Tom Brokaw

"The average man is more interested in a woman who is interested in him than he is in a woman—any woman—with beautiful legs."

—Marlene Dietrich

"A lady of forty-seven who has been married twenty-seven years and has six children knows what love really is and once described it for me like this: 'Love is what you've been through with somebody.' "

—James Thurber

"What love is a man can discover only at my age. . . . For me the world lives on for as long as the brain obeys the heart."

—Richard Wagner

"To be fifty not so long ago was to sigh resignedly at the loss of youth, beauty, energy, and, far worse, hope in the future. A woman who has chalked up the half-century today will find that youth—meaning gawky immaturity—is well lost, and that beauty has arrived at its true meaning."

—Anthony Burgess

"Now I find my dating pool is limited to men with gray hair, over fifty, who have a perverse attraction to wrinkles and varicosities."

—TERRYLYNN PEARSON

"I'm fifty now. I've reached the point where conceivably I could be making love to a woman and die in bed. That can happen. . . . As you get older, making love becomes more apocalyptic exactly because you're closer to the end of your life each time. As a result there's less desire to be promiscuous."

—NORMAN MAILER

"A man of fifty looks as old as Santa Claus to a girl of twenty."

—WILLIAM FEATHER

"What we are dealing with here is a concept of aging rather than a physiological fact. Women in their forties and fifties are as robust, as vital, as sexual as ever before in their lives—perhaps more so."

—ERICA JONG

"Every age has its admirers, ladies. While you, perhaps, are trading among the warmer climes of youth, there might be some to carry on a useful commerce in the frozen latitudes beyond fifty."

—OLIVER GOLDSMITH

"I believe that one's most passionate years are in the fifties. You have to decide not to sexually fade away."

—Helen Gurley Brown

"Can we not be stopped by age? Can we think there is allure? I don't know the answer yet. It's real cultural, but I'd love to change it a bit. A woman of fifty can be sexual and interesting and fabulous looking and at the top energy of her life."

—Faye Dunaway

Reprinted with permission from Hallmark Cards, Inc.

"All one's life as a young woman one is on show, a focus of attention, people notice you. You set yourself up to be noticed and admired. And then, not expecting it, you become middle-aged and anonymous. No one notices you. You achieve a wonderful freedom. It is a positive thing. You can move about, unnoticed and invisible."

—DORIS LESSING

"I live like a monk, almost. A monk with red lips, short dresses and big hair."

—TINA TURNER

In the eighties, *Playboy* magazine discovered that 50-year-old women could still display considerable sex appeal. Vikki La Motta (50 years old), Terry Moore (53), Mamie Van Doren (51), and Joan Collins (50) all posed at least seminude for photo layouts. The Joan Collins issue, with Collins also gracing the cover, reportedly was *Playboy*'s bestselling issue of the decade.

"Love is lame after fifty years."

—THOMAS HARDY

"With men, there's an element of sensuality and sexuality that we accept as they grow older. It all feeds into the myth of the father and the whole older man–younger girl thing. They do grow old, but we don't restrict our idea of what they can do."

—FAYE DUNAWAY

"At fifty, we learn that lust is underrated. Despite the warnings of pregnancy, disease and death, it leaves all other joys in the backfield. There is the possibility for perfect love—if one does not give up one's name or personal finances or place to live."

—KAREN DECROW

"I'm convinced that most middle-aged men aren't interested in involvements with very young women. It is not that sex has lost its power; if anything, the drive is stronger, because you know what you are doing at last, you have the accumulated sensations of a lifetime packed within you.

"But very few young women can join middle-aged men in the exacting voyage of a love affair, never mind embark on the ardent passage of a marriage. Sensible men know this. Unless they have recently emerged from monasteries, middle-aged men simply know too much for young women—about sex, about themselves, and about the world. . . . I couldn't bring myself to explain again who Sandy Koufax was."

—PETE HAMILL

"Most of the women I interviewed had a period where they felt down sexually in the late forties. Then they began to feel exhilarated in their fifties; secure in a deeper sexual identity as human beings in addition to feeling vital physically."

—GAIL SHEEHY

" 'A woman,' I said, 'should bear children for the state from her twentieth to her fortieth year; a man should beget them for the state from the time he passes his prime as a runner until he is fifty-five.' "

—PLATO

"I relate much better to women who are between thirty-five and fifty-five, because they know more about life, the way that I do, and we can talk about more varied subjects."

—OMAR SHARIF

● ● ● ● ●

About ten years ago, *50 Plus* magazine conducted a poll to determine how its readers defined "sex appeal" in the opposite sex. So pay attention to the results.

By a wide margin, women said that a man's eyes were the most important part of his body in determining sex appeal; the rest of his face came in a distant second. (Buttocks were down in sixth place, thank goodness.) Their ideal man was tall, blue-eyed, and clean-shaven, though opinion was pretty evenly divided over the virtues of hairy chests. (There appears not to have been a similar question regarding hairy backs.) By an overwhelming margin, women claimed to enjoy variety in lovemaking. Sex, they said, was best "anytime," preferably two or three times a week. Given the energy levels of most 50-year-old men, this no doubt explains why nearly 80 percent of women respondents said they would date a younger man if the opportunity presented itself. The leading "turn-ons" were listed as "smile, sensitivity, sense of humor, intelligence, and good listener," while such male qualities as "egotistical, domineering, poorly groomed, cheapskate, and chauvinistic" turned women off.

For their part, men identified a woman's breasts as the part of the body "most important to sex appeal"; face, legs, eyes, and buttocks came close behind in preference. Height and eye color were less critical than weight— overweight women were definitely viewed as less desirable—and long hair won out over short or curly locks. Ninety percent of the male respondents said they liked women to make the initial sexual advance in a rela- tionship, and over 80 percent enjoyed women who were sexually adventurous. Most men agreed that sex was fine anytime, though the number of men who said they thought sex would be great two or three times a week was only two-thirds the number of women who gave the same response. (And that was before the advent of ESPN and its round-the-clock sports programming.) Men rated person- ality, figure, smile, sense of humor, and intelligence as top "turn-ons," and said that they tended to avoid women who nagged or were bossy, poorly groomed, or over- weight.

"I feel if two people are in love, age difference doesn't matter. . . . I don't worry about gossip."
—MARY TYLER MOORE AT 51

"I'd love to be a father again. Friends tell me the ultimate joy is being a father after fifty-five."
—LARRY KING

"I think only kids who are very young should have sex, and people who aren't young should never get excited. After twenty-five, you should look, but never touch."

—ANDY WARHOL, who claimed to
be a virgin at 52

"I was fifty, matched with an ageing wife four years younger. It was time for me to stop lusting after brash girls."

—ANTHONY BURGESS

"There is some value in reading about what other people have done, but ultimately you have to do it yourself. It's like reading a Michelin guidebook. It tells you that there's a two-star restaurant in Paris and what kind of food is served there, but that's not the same as going there and tasting the food for yourself."

—DR. ALEX KATCHADOURIAN

"I'm fifty-three years old and six feet four. I've had three wives, five children and three grandchildren. I love good whiskey. I still don't understand women, and I don't think there is any man who does."

—JOHN WAYNE

FROM THE SIXTIES
TO THE
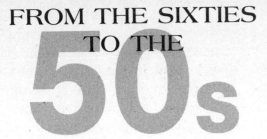
50s

All the rock stars, rebels, and counterculture idols from the sixties are either closing in on 50 or have already smashed through that barrier. Some have achieved the transition with grace, and others have refused to grow up. But most seem astonished to still be active at 50. His previous protestations notwithstanding, Mick Jagger is not only still singing "Satisfaction," but now he's a grandfather, too.

"I never thought I'd make it. I didn't think I'd get to be forty, to tell you the truth. Jeez, I feel like I'm a hundred million years old. Really, it's amazing. Mostly because it puts all the things I associate with my childhood so far back. . . .

"And I mean, here we are, we're getting into our fifties,

and where are these people who keep coming to our shows coming from? What do they find so fascinating about these middle-aged bastards playing basically the same thing we've always played? I mean, what do seventeen-year-olds find fascinating about this? . . . There must be a dearth of fun out there in America."

—JERRY GARCIA

"By the time I began my fiftieth year of life on August 30, 1984, I was out of Conifer Park and dried out from alcohol. My head was finally beginning to clear after nearly a quarter-century of substance abuse. . . .

"When you kick alcohol or junk, your senses are reawakened and heightened. The mind and body both undergo an amazing process of clarification. I heard and felt and smelled and saw life all over again. It was as if I had had bypass surgery and my arteries had been cleansed and opened wide. I was moved by a spirit of renewal and incredible luck."

—JOHN PHILLIPS, leader of the Mamas & Papas

"When I was eighteen, I had this image of a fifty-year-old as very mature, someone who knows all about life. But here I am turning fifty, and it's like starting all over. I'm supposed to be old and wise, but I'm less sure of life than ever before. I thought I would learn by now, but things keep hurting me, knocking me down. I think to myself, 'You mean, it doesn't get easier?' "

—YOKO ONO

"We killed the idea that guys heading for fifty were past producing worthwhile music in this idiom."

—BILL WYMAN

"I don't think I'd even think of [turning 50] very much if it wasn't for journalists. Because these *things,* these great milestones, they sort of come and go. The next day it's all over. It doesn't last very long. I think you *can* be quietly reflective about it. But I don't think it's too cathartic an experience."

—MICK JAGGER

"Mick [Jagger] will still be beautiful when he is fifty."

—PETE TOWNSEND

"Everyone can go, 'What? Jeez-us Curr-hrist! He's fifty! He isn't, is he! Bloody hell! That makes me old!' That's what they want. They want to use me as a gauge."

—PAUL McCARTNEY

"The thing that happens to musicians in middle age, especially if you've had a lot of success, a lot of attention, is that there comes a point when you either discover why you love music or it just becomes slick."

—PAUL SIMON

"I'm driving a lot of people crazy because I won't live in the past. You can get lost in the past or the future. You're not going to get anywhere that way, because you've already been there or you're not there yet. Me, I'm here right now."

—RINGO STARR AT 51

"My voice is better than ever, because of experience. At the risk of sounding egotistical—it just gets better. I am my favorite vocalist."

—ARETHA FRANKLIN

"But perhaps if I'd died before I got old, I might have been forgotten. You tend to hope you'll become James Dean or Jimi Hendrix, but a lot of dead people aren't remembered at all. So I haven't been able to achieve that one great ambition I had when I was nineteen. But I've tried to compensate by actually making myself happy."

—PETE TOWNSEND

"People just can't put the age fifty-two with a short skirt, the lipstick and wild hair."

—TINA TURNER

"You really do see the years, you really see the end. I think as long as you can crawl into the workshop, you should do the work. I always saw those old guys coming down to work, whatever job I happened to be in.

"Something about that always got to me. I'd like to be one of those old guys going to work."

—LEONARD COHEN

"Democracy is not something you believe in or a place you hang your hat, it's something you do. You participate. If you stop doing it, democracy crumbles."

—ABBIE HOFFMAN

Even after sixties-style revolution became unfashionable, former Yippie leader Abbie ("Don't trust anyone over thirty") Hoffman kept thumbing his nose at the establishment. At the age of 50, he managed to get himself arrested (along with Amy Carter) for trespassing while protesting a CIA recruitment drive at the University of Massachusetts. Subsequently, Abbie toured the nation urging the present generation of college students to get involved in political action. Two years later, at the age of 52, a disillusioned Hoffman apparently committed suicide by taking a massive dose of barbiturates.

"You can't go on doing that for years. I mean, just imagine having to sing 'Satisfaction' when you're forty-five."

—MARIANNE FAITHFULL

"When the baby-boom generation turns fifty, it will make a very loud noise—although some of the boomers might, for the first time in their lives, ask someone to turn the volume down a little."

—CHARLES GORDON

BOB DYLAN AT 50

Bob Dylan, the voice of a generation, turned 50 on May 24, 1991. He was on tour in South America at the time, and refused all requests for interviews on the subject of his birthday. "As far as he is concerned," declared Dylan's publicist (who, after all, must not have much to occupy his time, except for turning down requests for interviews), "it's just another day, and he certainly isn't planning a party."

On the other hand, Dylan made no attempt to hide his age. One music critic reported that "he certainly looks fifty. His face looks haggard, sort of puffy and bloated a bit, and he's skinny and wiry." And in the months preceding his 50th birthday, Dylan had delivered several pronouncements on what the approach of middle age meant to him. "You get older," he said, "you start having to get more family-oriented. You start having hopes for other people rather than for yourself. But I don't have nothin' to

complain about. I *did* it, you know? I did what I wanted
to do. . . .

"If I'm here at eighty, I'll be doing the same thing I'm
doing now. This is all I want to do—it's all I *can* do. . . . I
think I've always aimed my songs at people who I
imagined—maybe falsely so—had the same experiences
that I've had, who have kind of been through what I'd
been through."

Even though Dylan himself refused to have a party to
celebrate turning 50, several of his friends offered their
suggestions on appropriate presents for the greatest song-
writer of our time:

Arlo Guthrie: "A sense of humor."

Pete Seeger: "A little peace and quiet and an invisible
cloak that would enable him to go wherever he wanted
without being hassled."

Mick Jagger: "After seeing him on the Grammy Awards,
I'd get him a new hat and a good song."

Judy Collins: "A pair of sneakers."

Dave Stewart: "I wouldn't want to give him anything. I
once gave him an antique Gibson acoustic guitar in im-
maculate condition, and he lost it."

Bill Graham: "For his body of work—a Nobel Prize for
Literature."

Johnny Cash: "Peace of mind."

Barbara Orbison: "A big hug, a new van, and a pink
tutu."

Roger McGuinn: "Fifty dimes and fifty tambourines."

Ray Davies: "A new birth certificate, so that he could go
through it all again and give us another golden era full
of great songs."

T-Bone Burnett: "I would arrange it so that he never had to be included in any more lists."

                Source: *The Independent* (May 5, 1991)

YOUR BODY AT 50

You may as well face the facts. There are a number of physical changes that set in around the age of 50 (if not before), and there doesn't seem to be much you can do about most of them.

According to Bill Cosby, it all starts "when the body calls a meeting with the brain and tells it what it is not going to do anymore." By the time you turn 50, your bones have stopped growing and have actually started to shrink. Supporting muscles and ligaments become lax; back troubles increase as your discs get squeezed out of position. Your reflexes slow down, though not by much. Most men notice that the strength of their hand grip has declined precipitously between the ages of 40 and 50.

Presbyopia sets in as the lenses of your eyes grow less elastic, which you notice especially at close range, and so reading glasses or bifocals become necessary. Your speaking voice has risen from a C to an E-flat, and you cannot hear certain high-pitched noises. Your earlobes are longer and fatter, your skull is thicker, and your memory seems to be deteriorating. But even though you may have developed a case of Dunlap's disease (as in, "Uh-oh, my stomach dunlapped over my belt"), your waist may well have reached its maximum size by the time you turn 50.

Women at age 50 tend to show more of a tendency to grow fat than their male counterparts, and the extra tissue collects around the waist. Breasts droop as gravity exerts its inexorable pull, sleep lines carve deeper furrows across the face, and 50 years of cramming feet into tight shoes inevitably leads to aching feet. Although vigorous exercise can forestall some of the physical effects of age until you turn 50, it has less power to prevent them after that age, though it is true that fitness levels in active women decline less precipitously than in their more sedentary friends.

All of these changes can produce in both sexes a condition known popularly as dysmorphophobia: an intense but unfounded fear of looking ugly. Certainly it has produced a bonanza for the plastic surgery industry in America. According to statistics compiled by the American Society of Plastic and Reconstructive Surgeons, nearly 60 percent of the facelifts performed annually in this country are done on women between the ages of 51 and 64. As Chad Gordon, a sociologist at Rice University, put it, "Aging sucks. It's filled with all those D words—decay, decrepitude, degeneration, dying. . . . Then there's balding, paunchiness, losing sex drives and capabilities, back trouble, headaches, cholesterol and high blood pressure—they all go from the far horizon to close up. Then you worry about worrying about all those things."

Reprinted with permission from Hallmark Cards, Inc.

Besides, honesty has its own rewards. When you reach 50, you know what it takes to survive, and you can admire the visible symbols of accomplishment in the faces of those around you. As the London *Daily Mail* pointed out nearly 50 years ago, "There is a case for keeping wrinkles. They are the long-service stripes earned in the hard campaign of life. . . . A wrinkled face is a firm face, a steady face, a safe face. Wrinkles are the dried-up riverbeds of a lifetime's tears, the nostalgic remnants of a million smiles. Wrinkles are the crannies and footholds on the smooth visage of life on which man can cling and gain some comfort and security."

• • • • •

"Nature gives you the face you have at twenty; it is up to you to merit the face you have at fifty."

—GABRIELLE "COCO" CHANEL

"In a man's middle years there is scarcely a part of the body he would hesitate to turn over to the proper authorities."

—E. B. WHITE

"When you get past fifty, you have to decide whether to keep your face or your figure. I kept my face."

—BARBARA CARTLAND

"I'm forty-nine but I could be twenty-five except for my face and my legs."

—NADINE GORDIMER

"One thing about me is flourishing: my fingernails."

—BETTY COMDEN

"I am in better shape at fifty than I was at fifteen, when I lugged around some extra pounds of flab and most likely would have collapsed before finishing an hour of singles tennis in ninety-degree heat."

—JANE BRODY

"I always think that as you get older, you always look better with a little flesh."

—POLLY BERGEN

Some Birthday Riddles
For Your 50ᵀᴴ Birthday

Q How many 50-year-olds does it take to change a lightbulb?

A None. They prefer it dark. Better for napping.

Q Why did the 50-year-old cross the road?

A A scout was there to help.

Q What do you call a 50-year-old with a good sex life?

A Liar.

Happy 50ᵗʰ!

Reprinted with permission from Hallmark Cards, Inc.

"What is wrong with looking like you remember Harry James, have borne a few children, suffered a few sunburns, shed more than a few tears, and known more than a few sleepless nights? When I see *that* face—I think it's Glenda Jackson's—when I switch on the news or a TV series, I will know the revolution has arrived. On that happy day, the phrase 'She's showing her age' will be greeted as a compliment; and 'She doesn't look her age' with what it deserves. A 'So what?' "

—MARY CANTWELL

"You know, when you turn fifty, you're supposed to go have a complete physical. I did, and, when the nurse asked how tall I was, I said 'six-six.' She said, 'Why don't we see?' So she measured me, and I was six-six and one-half. I'm still growing!"

—TOMMY TUNE

"He was tired; his nervous energy ran low; and, like a horse that wears out, he quitted the race course, left the stable, and sought pastures as far as possible from the old."

—HENRY ADAMS AT 50

"At fifty, you believe you can still climb Mount McKinley, but then why does your doctor react with an expression of bemused contempt? It's the male equivalent of the biological clock ticking away. A grandfather clock."

—TOM BROKAW

"It would be disastrous if men were physically old in their fifties, as they used to be, but it is an even greater loss if most of them lose their intellectual and spiritual energy by that age."

—SIR RICHARD LIVINGSTONE

"The things that worry me, that get me down, are the things that worry all middle-aged Americans. What am I doing to do when I get arthritis? Diabetes? When the first heart attack comes? The hospital bills are going to cost $30,000, and I don't have medical insurance."

—ABBIE HOFFMAN

"At a certain age, a man is like an athlete. One of the reasons I got out of sports is that I could see what it was going to bring—when the muscles don't work anymore and the bones begin to act up. You reach a point where you haven't developed something for yourself. You're doomed. It's like some kind of weird purgatory."

—ROBERT REDFORD

"Middle age is when your age starts to show around your middle."

—BOB HOPE

"What I fear, far more than selling out, is wearing out."

—NORMAN MAILER

"It's the decomposition that gets me. You spend your whole life looking after your body. And then you rot away, like that."

—BRIGITTE BARDOT

"We no longer look forward to letting go at thirty. There is no thought of aging gracefully at forty. At fifty, we are faced with a prospect of daily regiments to soften our skin and tighten our thighs. The end prospect of all this is that those of us who failed to look like Brooke Shields at seventeen can now fail to look like Victoria Principal at thirty-three, like Linda Evans at forty-one and like Sophia Loren at fifty."

—ELLEN GOODMAN

"Dr. Joyce Brothers says that I'm not getting older, I'm getting better. This is the kind of doctor that inspires a second opinion. I will settle for being just slightly worse, a few steps slower and a bit more out of focus."

—RALPH SCHOENSTEIN

"This is foolish vanity. Youth is no longer essential or even becoming. Rapidly approaching fifty-seven, health and happiness are more important than lissomeness. To be fat and bald is slovenly, unless it is beyond your control, but however slim you get you will still be the age you are and no one will be fooled, so banish this nonsense once and for all, conserve your vitality by eating enough and enjoying it."

—NOEL COWARD

"I seem to have a body that can't deal with more than one meal a day."

—STEPHANIE POWERS

"I try not to eat after 5 P.M."

—JANE FONDA

"I don't allow myself to be pressured anymore. I try to keep the work balanced so I don't get stressed out. And I make sure I find time for myself when there is no one else around."

—Nancy Wilson

"I don't exercise. I don't spend much money on clothes. Of course I care about how I look. But if I have to spend more than fifteen minutes in the morning, I'm not going to do it. There are more important things to do."

—Gloria Steinem

"I am fifty now and I'm tired. My hair is falling out and the highlight of my day is a nap, and the water flows from a small ravine in my stomach after a shower."

—Bill Cosby

INTERVIEW WITH
ELLEN GOODMAN

Ellen Goodman, nationally syndicated columnist for the *Boston Globe*, recently turned 50, and was kind enough to share her thoughts on the subject with me.

Q: In some of your columns, you have written that everyone now is trying to make us think that we can look like Jane Fonda or Sophia Loren at fifty. Do you think our society has trouble dealing with the aging process?

A: Well, I suspect we will have less and less trouble as the baby-boom generation gets to middle age, because they tend to make a trend out of everything, and a positive out of everything. I noticed the *Atlantic Monthly* this month has an upbeat piece on midlife, which seemed to me to be a sort of baby-boom advance guard.

Q: And that's what Gloria Steinem said back in the

eighties, that fifty is what forty used to be. Is that true? Are we pushing back that age barrier?

A: Yes. Lots of things are happening simultaneously. On the one hand, people are often younger and healthier at fifty than, say, our grandparents' generation. On the other hand, a lot of people are actually living the lives at fifty that their parents were living at forty. In other words, their children are younger—this is not true for me personally— but they had children later, they're hitting their career peaks later, because of difficulty getting into their career tracks, or just taking time out.

So, on the one hand, people are feeling younger physically at fifty. On the other hand, they're also leading lives that were more like what forty-year-olds led a generation ago.

Q: What effect do all these advertisements have, that try to get people to look younger forever? Do they have an effect on our mental outlook toward aging?

A: I think there is still a terrible imperative for women to look young. If you read the Helen Gurley Brown book, it's quite extraordinary. She keeps saying that you should do *anything* to look young. And it's depressing.

Q: It is, isn't it?

A: I think most women of my generation in midlife are sort of caught by two attitudes. One is the societal attitude that they have to look young, and that's often translated into a very pragmatic economic imperative to look younger—that looking younger is "professional," the way being thinner is "professional." You see that all the way from the flight attendants scandals to how difficult it is for women to get jobs with a future after they hit fifty.

At the same time, I think there's a real internal sensibility that's grown among women that they want to accept and not fight age. They want to accept themselves, and not be victims of these imperatives.

These are two principles that are very active, particularly in the lives of midlife women, but also to an extent among men in midlife, because after all, a lot of the men are now under what was once an exclusively female imperative to look young.

Q: That's right. Do you think men and women really approach this differently? I've found that men have a harder time with forty, and women have more trouble with thirty or thirty-five, and fifty.

A: How old are you?

Q: I'm forty-two.

A: My sense, having been through forty and fifty with a lot of men that I know, is that that is not accurate. Fifty is a jolt too, and it varies from man to man. Maybe forty is the first time that men realize they're not going to be president of the United States. But a lot of men—at fifty, the physical side hits them, the sense that they're not going to hit the ball out of the park, and assorted other athletic metaphors.

Q: Well, see, that's already hit me. That got me at forty. I've also found that in many other cultures, women receive a tremendous amount of respect when they hit fifty, when they are considered to have accumulated the wisdom of the tribe.

A: Yes. I think there are a lot of people talking about that. I was at a conference at Radcliffe a few weeks ago for women over fifty, and there were a lot of people talking very much about how when you turn fifty, you might as well say whatever you think. And a lot of women are somewhat freer as primary caretaker at fifty, although that is sort of a myth, too. That, I think, is more of a myth as our mothers live longer, and that in fact at fifty a lot of women are switching from being working mothers to being working daughters.

But I think there is some sense when you hit fifty of "If I'm not going to speak my mind now, when am I?" But that's never been a particular problem to me, because I do it professionally.

Q: Did you have any trouble turning fifty?

A: Not really. I was conscious of it. I had a wonderful small dinner party for my five closest women friends and their respective partners, and it was very warm. I felt surrounded by people who—I think when you're fifty, you have a sense of being surrounded by a group of people that you've nurtured, either friends or family. And that you've really created the life that you're leading, and if you're happy with that life, it can be a very solid time.

And that's always the truth, isn't it? If you're happy with your life, it's pretty good.

Q: Sure, that's true at any age. I also assume that at forty or fifty, you realize that if there are things you haven't yet done, now is the time to do them, which accounts for some of the shifts that people make at this stage of the game.

A: Yes, but I think the shift is probably overemphasized. The midlife crisis has been way overblown. I think that there is some solidifying that goes on between forty and fifty, too, as well as that sense of it being the last chance to catch the A train. At fifty, too, women have a real marker, which is menopause, which is often looked at negatively by people. But it also marks a transition, it's an official biological marker that you can hang your hat on. You can say, This is the end of childbearing. It may have been fifteen years or twenty since you had your last child, but this is the first day of the rest of your life.

Q: So you think the whole concept of a midlife crisis is overblown?
A: I do.

Q: Do you think we make too much of these decade milestones?
A: No, I don't think it's a bad idea to mark a moment in your life. It's a little bit like having a party or a celebration. I generally approve of celebrating with people, and marking things, and not letting things go unnoticed. I tend to be in favor of paying attention to certain markers.

Q: A chance to take stock and see what you've done and what you want to do?
A: Or just to celebrate.

Q: Okay. There's not enough of that, is there?
A: Well, I think it's always good for people to gather together in a society that doesn't have a lot of official rites of passage. We don't have all those celebrations. We make our own, and one of the ways we do it is by gathering together and having birthday parties.

There are other things. Do you know Carly Simon's birthday song? There's one great line in there where she says—oh, I can't remember it now, it's down the memory hole. And I can't even say that's because I've turned fifty, it was always down the memory hole. I tell my daughter, don't let them take me away because my memory's shot; it's always been shot.

And somewhere in this area, if you want to peg it to turning fifty, I think it's important to stop running for the sake of running.

Q: Which means what?
A: To stop simply filling in the calendar for every minute. To take a little time out. This may be the lament of somebody whose life is extremely busy, but it's the time to think about overload, and also to think about what it is that makes life enjoyable, rather than just putting one foot in front of the other.

One other thing. When I turned fifty, I started telling people my age. Not that I was hiding it before, but I mean actively telling people my age.

Q: Why?
A: As a kind of a political statement. It was really interesting. I would fold it into a comment after a speech or an answer. I'd say, "I'm fifty and . . ." or "I'm fifty-one, and . . ." People are very surprised when you tell your age in any overt public way. I think it's an important sort of thing to do, because it's breaking a barrier, particularly when you are over fifty. The cliché is that women don't tell their age, and when they do tell their age, they're asking you to say, "Oh, you don't look fifty." But to just lay it out there—I've noticed that from the reaction.

Q: What advice do you have for someone who is turning fifty?

A: Have a good time. I mean it. Have a good time.

ATHLETES AT 50

Professional athletes at 50 are few and far between. Remarkably, hockey superstar Gordie Howe was still playing for the Hartford Whalers in the National Hockey League at the age of 52. Jockey Willie Shoemaker won his fourth Kentucky Derby when he was 54, and in recent years several over-50 race-car drivers—notably Harry Gant and Mario Andretti—have won major races on their circuits. Former light-heavyweight boxing champion Archie Moore continued to fight professionally until the age of 52, until he finally retired in 1965; more than two decades later, Moore served as an inspiration for George Foreman's vaunted comeback.

Although the oldest person ever to win an Olympic medal was a couple of years shy of his 50th birthday—Tebbs Lloyd-Johnson, who at 48 captured a bronze metal in the 50,000-meter walk in the 1948 London Olympics—

there is plenty of room in amateur athletics for men and women who have turned 50. Gentlemen over 50 are eligible for the Men's Senior Baseball League, the only nationwide master's baseball league in the United States. With more than 20,000 players on 1,400 teams in over 100 cities, the MSBL (fondly known as the "Men's Big Stomach and Butts League," since most of the participants are in less than optimum physical condition) sponsors a six-month season. Most of the games are held on Sunday afternoons, and each fall the nation's best teams meet in the league's own World Series, usually held in a nice warm climate to keep pulled muscles to a minimum.

Both men and women are eligible to join the Amateur Athletic Union's master's division for basketball. Teams are grouped both by sex and age (at 5-year intervals, from 35 to 64), and by skill levels. Be warned that the competition in these leagues can be fierce. According to Dr. Williams Bosworth, head of the master's division, "It's a bloody battle even when the sixty-year-olds get out on the court and fight for position."

Anyone searching for a more relaxed athletic environment may wish to consider the United States Tennis Association's senior division, where players 50 and older—more than half of whom are women—compete only in doubles matches from late spring through summer. And for those who still long to sprint and hurdle across the track, be advised that the Amateur Athletic Union's master's division begins at age 40 for men and 35 for women. Meets include all standard track and field events, and some runners are still extremely proficient even at 50. Men in their late forties have been known to run the 100-meter dash in just over 11 seconds, only slightly more than a second off the best time of Olympic champion Carl Lewis.

But running has always been a favorite pastime of over-50 athletes. In fact, Sam Snead once claimed that "the only way a golfer can really stay in shape is to do a lot of running."

"Do you run, Sam?" he was asked.

"Only," Snead replied, "if somebody's chasin' me."

● ● ● ● ●

"When I was forty my doctor advised me that a man in his forties shouldn't play tennis. I heeded his advice carefully and could hardly wait until I reached fifty to start again."

—HUGO BLACK

"I'm forty-nine and I want to live to be fifty."

—EDDIE SAWYER, following his resignation as manager of the Philadelphia Phillies

"Fifty is young for a tree, midlife for an elephant, and ancient for a quarter-miler, whose son now says, 'Dad, I just can't run the quarter with you anymore unless I bring something to read.' "

—BILL COSBY

"It's obvious I'm closer to fifty than I am to twenty. But I'm productive. People who are fifty or sixty have to realize they don't need to live with fear. I had the fear. I broke out of it."

—GEORGE FOREMAN

"I'll win the heavyweight championship back when I'm fifty years old! Isn't that something? Is that powerful? They can pay $20 million or $50 million to whoever I fight, Holyfield or Tyson. This is gonna shake 'em up. It's like a miracle, a dream. Muhammad Ali is back! Can you picture this?

"Can you believe it? Dancin' at fifty! ... Ooooohhh.... Dancin' at fifty. Maaannnnn. It'll be bigger than the moon shot! I'm dedicatin' the fight to the baby boomers, the people who were six years old when I beat Sonny Liston. Now they're thirty-four. I'll do the Ali shuffle!"

—MUHAMMAD ALI

Although few jockeys in the world of thoroughbred racing compete at the Triple Crown level after the age of 50, Willie Shoemaker captured the Kentucky Derby in 1986, shortly after his 54th birthday. At 50, "the Shoe" already had become only the second jockey in the history of American racing to receive the prestigious Eclipse Award of Merit, voted for his "extraordinary accomplishments as a jockey" and for "being an outstanding good-will ambassador for racing."

Shoemaker's extraordinary accomplishments seemed to amaze even himself. "I was fifty-three and still riding," he marveled. "In the jockeys' room, I felt like a grandfather. In fact, I was a grandfather." A year later, during his Derby-winning season, Shoemaker won twenty-eight more stakes events, bringing in over $5 million in earnings.

Meanwhile, on the race-car circuit, 53-year-old Mario Andretti became the oldest man ever to win an Indy car race when he captured the Valvoline 200 at Phoenix International Raceway in April 1993. Andretti's performance was matched only by that of Harry Gant, the erstwhile house builder and grandfather from Taylorsville, North Carolina, who put together a string of three straight Winston Cup wins in the late summer of 1991. Following his third victory, an unprecedented feat for any driver over 50, Gant's racing team handed out buttons that read, "Life Begins at 51."

"I'm proud to be fifty-one years old," Gant told reporters. "A lot of people didn't live to be fifty-one, so I appreciate where I am." Gant claimed that the savvy that came from five decades had nothing to do with his success—"I can't tell the difference from when I was forty or thirty," he said. "I'm still doing it just the same"—but his opponents disagreed strongly. "We're just like a bunch of high school boys chasing a pro," complained Michael Waltrip.

Certainly Gant proved that at 51 he was better able to face the psychological pressures of life in the really fast lane. "When I was younger, I was dead set on winning," he observed. "I'd feel bad, not sleep at night, run things through my mind. I've learned to block it out when I leave a race, and flip it back on for practice. I don't get mad when things don't go good. I don't get excited when I don't win. It makes it a lot easier for people to live with me." And to prove it, he celebrated his achievement by going home and building an addition onto his garage.

"If things keep going like this," Gant confided, "I could keep it [going] until I'm fifty-five or fifty-six."

"I blew past my fiftieth birthday in 1962," noted golfer Sam Snead, "barely taking time to snuff out the candles on my cake. The pro tour had grown to almost $2 million in prize money—about twenty times more than when I'd started a quarter century-earlier. I'd won the World Cup individual title in 1961 [at age 49], plus the Sam Snead Festival and the Tournament of Champions, and I figured to collect a few more coins in the years to come. Besides, I was having fun bumping heads with a whole new generation of golfers—Palmer, Casper, Player, Littler, and a youngster who'd just jumped on the carousel, a kid named Nicklaus. It was no time to leave the party."

More than any other sport, professional golf provides a format for athletes over 50 to continue to display their skills and earn substantial prize money. In the late seventies, a match-play tournament known as The Legends of Golf, featuring famous golfers who were still active but no longer competitive on the regular PGA circuit, made its debut on national television. When the ratings proved surprisingly robust, a contingent of veteran golfers led by Sam Snead and Julius Boros convinced PGA Commissioner Deane Beman to launch a senior tour, reserved for players who had passed their 50th birthday.

Success followed swiftly. In its first year, 1980, the Senior PGA Tour featured only two tournaments, with total prize money worth $250,000; by 1985, there were twenty-seven events worth more than $6 million. As Snead and Boros faded from the scene, Arnold Palmer, Gary Player, and Chi Chi Rodriguez joined the tour and generated even greater fan interest.

Competition among the golfers grew increasingly fierce. When Lee Trevino turned 50 in 1990, he played like a man possessed, winning nearly $1.2 million in a single year. From those early years when many players on the tour were frankly out of shape (Jack Nicklaus referred to them disparagingly as "round-bellies"), the quality of play has increased substantially. Nowadays the Senior Tour has its own fitness trailer, which is frequently crowded to capacity. The players are having such a good time—and earning so much money—that they want to stay around for as long as possible. "A lot of the guys playing out there now aren't going anywhere," confided Beman. "Golfers stay around a long time. They have great players out here, and great competition. Most of them are not as good as they were in their prime, but who cares?"

"There's a reason the fans love this tour," explained Trevino. "These guys were their heroes they grew up with. These are the guys who won all the biggies. And most of 'em haven't lost a step . . . It's the greatest thing that's ever happened to golf. It's paradise out there."

Yet there are still a few golfers who find it hard to adjust to turning 50, and Jack Nicklaus has been the most prominent example in recent years. Although he had not won a major tournament since capturing the 1986 Masters at the age of 46, Nicklaus derided the quality of play on the PGA Seniors Tour. "The problem for me," Nicklaus complained, "is that the guys who are competing are the same guys I have beaten for thirty years."

Nevertheless, Nicklaus joined the Senior Tour and promptly rediscovered the swing that had deserted him three years earlier. Later, Jack admitted that "turning 50 was the best thing that ever happened to me from a golf standpoint. I knew my golf game wasn't in shape, and if it wasn't, these guys would have run me right down the road. They would have laughed me right out of here. I had to be ready for that."

Still, Nicklaus remained sensitive about his age, even though he made an excellent run at the Masters title again in 1993, at the age of 53, finishing in the top ten on the last day of the tournament. "Why would it be so phenomenal for me to win here at fifty-three?" Jack asked reporters after leading the field after eighteen holes. "I just don't see where age has a whole lot to do with it."

"Fifty is not a tough year. As for Jack [Nicklaus] resisting it, the alternative is a lot worse."

—ARNOLD PALMER

"I went to bed [on September 4] and I was old and washed up. I woke up a rookie. What could be better?"

—RAYMOND FLOYD, on joining the
PGA Senior Tour on
his 50th birthday

"My grandmother lived to 114 and my grandfather to 110, and that was on my father's side. On my mother's side, both my grandparents were over 100 when they died. One of my uncles was 108 when he died, even though he claimed he was 83 but that was because he had 19 wives and 79 kids. Not wives, really, concubines. So at 55, I'm really middle-aged."

—CHI CHI RODRIGUEZ

50

FACTS

1. There are currently more than sixty-three million Americans age 50 and over, nearly twice as many as there were in 1950.

2. Connie Mack is the only man who managed major league baseball teams for 50 years, from 1901 to 1950.

3. Clementine Churchill took up skiing at the age of 50, and became positively addicted to the sport.

4. Prince Philip, on the other hand, gave up polo at 50, and started racing horse-drawn carriages.

5. Contrary to the popular image of middle-aged men divorcing their wives to run away with nubile 20-year-old girls, men over the age of 45 usually marry women who are only 3.6 to 6.9 years younger.

6. Kurt Vonnegut wrote his seventh novel, *Breakfast of Champions*, as "a kind of fiftieth-birthday present" to himself. The book, illustrated with Vonnegut's own doodles with a felt-tip pen, represented an attempt to come to terms with his despair over what he perceived as an ever-widening cultural vacuum in the United States.

7. In 1962, Newsweek magazine called Richard Nixon "a political has-been at the age of 49." Six years later, he won the 1968 presidential election.

8. After the age of 50, your sense of smell starts to become less keen. This undoubtedly explains why your grandmother always seemed to be wearing too much perfume, unless she was just trying to irritate you.

9. Back in the eighties, a doctor in San Antonio, Texas, launched a newsletter entitled *Sex Over Forty*, dedicated to the proposition that "sex over 50 . . . has the potential for being the most rewarding sex of all." Each month, the newsletter provided information on such topics as "Impotence: 11 ways to tell whether it's physical or purely psychological," "How you and your mate can play with those middle-of-the-night opportunities," "The story of one man's penile implant," and "Multiple orgasms: how to achieve them over forty, even if you've never before."

10. Walter B. Pitkin was already 54 years old when he wrote his bestselling book *Life Begins at Forty*.

11. Those 50 and older control more than half of all the discretionary income in the United States. And if you add their net worth, the sixty-three million Americans over 50 hold a staggering $7 trillion, more than two-thirds of the nation's net worth.

12. Tommy Chong (of Cheech and Chong fame) turned 50 on the downslide, two years after his breakup with Richard "Cheech" Marin. On a more optimistic note, Pete Rose was already out of jail—where he had served five months for income tax evasion—by the time he turned 50.

13. Elizabeth Taylor holds the celebrity record for most marriages (seven) by the age of 50.

14. There is an entrepreneur named "Uncle Bernie" in Roanoke, Virginia, who would like you to enroll in his "50 Plus Wholesale Club" today! If you do, he will send you an electric sandwich-maker for only $13.

15. At the age of 49, former New York mayor John Lindsay was voted the sexiest man in the world in a London newspaper poll.

16. Middle-aged settlers in colonial America used the juice of green pineapples to erase wrinkles.

17. On the eve of her 50th birthday, ballerina Margot Fonteyn was still mesmerizing audiences in her role as the teenaged Juliet. Another well-known ballerina, Natalia Makarova, made her dramatic stage debut at the age of 50.

18. Very few opera singers are able to maintain their talents after they turn 50. Joan Sutherland, Birgit Nilsson, and Leontyne Price are the outstanding exceptions.

19. Any 50-year-old electric bass players looking for a job should consult the Rolling Stones, who finally fired Bill Wyman in early 1993.

20. Back in the thirties, Dr. Robert G. Jackson claimed to have been physically "reborn" at the age of 50 through a philosophy of "natural health through natural living habits leading to a natural immunity to disease." For five dollars, he offered to send readers a copy of his book, *How to Be Always Well,* so they, too, could "do anything the average twenty-two-year-old can do *and do it better.*"

21. Jane Russell began filming commercials for Playtex bras shortly after her 50th birthday.

22. For some reason, *Modern Maturity* magazine reported in the *New York Times* that "people over 50 are every bit as likely to invest in home furnishings and remodeling as any other age group." Who cares?

23. The Nintendo Corporation recently launched an advertising campaign aimed at men between the ages of 18 and 49. Just wait until Super Mario turns 50; then they'll be sorry.

24. By the year 2000, there will be thirty-two million Americans between the ages of 50 and 60.

25. Guides for job-hunting after 50 recommend that you avoid the use of phrases such as "At my age . . ." "Back when I was younger . . ." and "Listen, son . . ." during job interviews.

26. Comedienne Fanny Brice was still performing her Baby Snooks routine on the radio at the age of 50. Unfortunately, Brice refused to wear glasses while performing, for fear of spoiling Snooks's appearancé to radio audiences, so her writers had to provide her with a script in triple-size type.

27. The television show *Middle Age* flopped miserably during a brief run in 1991. "The name was a colossal mistake," admitted producer Stan Rogow. " 'Middle-age' is this horrible-sounding thing you've heard throughout your life and hated." Better to watch *The Golden Girls,* so you would know what you had to look forward to. Besides, those women were *so much older* than you.

28. After five years of publishing, *50-Plus* magazine changed its name to *New Choices for the Best Years.*

29. Fifty-three percent of Americans between the ages of 45 and 59 prefer to spend their leisure time at home. Twenty-six percent of people in the same age bracket go to bed before midnight on New Year's Eve.

30. Jerry Garcia, leader of the Grateful Dead, restored his health and lost sixty pounds at the age of 50 on a special vegetarian diet: "No oil, no fat, no salt, nothing with a face."

31. A recent study revealed that nearly half of the divorced women between ages 50 and 59 prefer to remain single, rather than lose their independence in a second marriage.

32. Foot-care advice for people over 50: Keep your feet clean, change socks frequently, and always dry the skin between the toes completely to reduce moisture and keep down fungi.

33. The average score on IQ tests for 50-year-olds is 100, compared to 111 at age 30.

34. Researchers now believe that people between the ages of 40 and 60 lose a substantial number of cells in the part of brain that registers anxiety, a phenomenon that would make you not give a damn that you no longer look as young as you once did. So while tummy tucks and hair transplants are popular among American women and men in their forties, few such operations are performed on patients who have already turned 50.

35. A recent poll disclosed that the favorite forms of recreation for people in their fifties are fishing, walking, golf, tennis, and swimming.

36. Several weeks after his 50th birthday, King George III of England suffered a mysterious illness and went quite mad. For the rest of his life, he was plagued with recurring bouts of insanity.

37. If you lived in ancient Sparta, you would still be in the army and living in the barracks at the age of 50. You did not receive your discharge until the age of 60.

38. Experts estimate that Medicare reserves will be depleted between 1998 and 2000. Uh-oh.

39. Shortly after she turned 55, Zsa Zsa Gabor got married for the sixth time.

40. Sore muscles and tender joints account for almost one-third of all doctor visits for people over the age of 50.

41. Michael Todd was 50 years old when he married 24-year-old Elizabeth Taylor.

42. When asked to complete the sentence, "You aren't middle-aged until . . . ," a random sampling of 1,200 Americans replied, ". . . you don't recognize the names of the music groups on radio" and ". . . it takes a day or two longer to recover from strenuous exercise."

43. In World War I, over 650,000 50-year-old American males registered for the draft. I have no idea why.

44. Top models throughout the world are discovering that there is life after 50. At the age of 50, Catherine Deneuve will be the top model for a new line of skin-care products from Yves Saint Laurent. And Cheryl Tiegs recently signed a five-year modeling contract that will take her almost to her 50th birthday.

45. You may be deluged with phone calls from mutual-funds salespeople who are waiting to sell you all sorts of products after you turn 50, on the theory that people first start to think seriously about retirement when they reach that age.

46. Back in 1971, Pan Am ran an advertisement offering special summer rates for customers who were 50 years old—"Because that's the time when we come to understand what getting older really means. We find ourselves remembering not so much what we did with our life, but what we didn't do with it." Thanks, guys.

47. An Apparel Sizing Project for Women 55 and Older has been established by the American Society of Testing and Materials and the Institute of Standards Research. The project's objective is to gather data on the changes in size and shape that occur after a woman reaches the age of 55. "We need to break down the notion that women simply get bigger as they get older," explained the codirector of the project.

48. Abraham Lincoln did not grow a beard until he was 52 years old.

49. At the age of 53, Tina Turner confided that she follows a diet of steamed vegetables and Thai food to maintain her figure; Raquel Welch, on the other hand, uses daily yoga, vitamins, meditation, and exercise.

50. At 50, you are too old to enter the CIA's clandestine career training program. They probably figure you'll forget the secret code.

Plume

WILD & WITTY

Plume

COMIC RELIEF